Ibn Kammūna's Examination of the Three Faiths

PUBLISHED UNDER THE AUSPICES
OF THE NEAR EASTERN CENTER
UNIVERSITY OF CALIFORNIA, LOS ANGELES

# *Ibn Kammūna's Examination of the Three Faiths*

A THIRTEENTH-CENTURY ESSAY IN
THE COMPARATIVE STUDY OF RELIGION
TRANSLATED FROM THE ARABIC,
WITH AN INTRODUCTION AND NOTES

*by Moshe Perlmann*



UNIVERSITY OF CALIFORNIA PRESS
BERKELEY LOS ANGELES LONDON 1971

University of California Press
Berkeley and Los Angeles, California

University of California Press, Ltd.
London, England



ISBN: 0–520–01658–0
Library of Congress Catalog Card Number: 73–102659
Printed in the United States of America

Designed by Dave Comstock

Genesis 37:16

# *Translator's Note*

IT is my pleasant duty to acknowledge the advice of Professors David H. Baneth, Herbert Davidson, Leon Nemoy, Josef Van Ess, and Harry A. Wolfson, on which I was able to draw in the course of preparing the Arabic edition issued in 1967 as well as the present translation—particularly in connection with Chapter I. Professor Milton Anastos read the proofs of Chapter III. Dr. Aaron Haddad and Dr. Charles Wendell were kind enough to read respectively the Arabic and English proofs.

I am grateful to Mrs. Theresa Joseph and to my wife, Mrs. Ida Perlmann, for their help in editing the translation, and to Miss Barbara Zimmerman for her skill and understanding in seeing the book through the press.

The following publishers have put me under obligation by permitting quotations from their publications:

T. & T. Clark, Edinburgh (*The Qur'an*, translated by Richard Bell, 1937–1939);

George Allen and Unwin, Ltd., London (*Faith and Practice of Al-Ghazali*, by W. Montgomery Watt; Series in Ethical and Religious Classics of East and West, 1953);

John Murray, London (*Avicenna on Theology*, Wisdom of the East Series, 1951).

M. P.

# *Abbreviations*

| | |
|---|---|
| *Ahwal* | Ibn Sīnā, *Aḥwāl al-Nafs,* ed. A. F. al-Ahwānī (Cairo, 1952); previous ed. H. Z. Ülken, in Ibn Sina Risaleleri II (Istanbul, 1953). |
| *Arba'īn* | Muḥammad Ibn 'Umar, Fakhr al-Din al-Rāzī, *Kitāb al-Arba'īn fī uṣūl al-dīn.* Hyderabad, 1353/1935. |
| Bukhārī | Bukhārī, *al-Ṣaḥīḥ: Le Recueil des Traditions mahométanes.* Vols. I–IV, ed. L. Krehl and Th. W. Juynboll. Leiden, 1862–1908. |
| *De Anima* | Avicenna, *De Anima, Being the Psychological Part of Kitāb al-Shifā',* ed. F. Rahman. London, 1959. |
| *EI* | *Encyclopaedia of Islam.* Leiden, 1913–1938. |
| *EI*[2] | *Encyclopaedia of Islam.* New ed. Leiden, 1960–. |
| *GAL* | Carl Brockelmann, *Geschichte der Arabischen Litteratur.* 2d ed. 5 vols. Leiden, 1937–1943. |
| *Guide* | Maimonides, *Dalālat al-Ḥā'irīn: Le Guide des égarés,* ed. S. Munk. Paris, 1856–1866; *The Guide for the Perplexed,* trans. M. Friedlander. New York, 1956 (orig. 1904); *The Guide of the Perplexed,* trans. Sh. Pines. Chicago, 1963. |
| Ibn Ḥanbal | Ibn Ḥanbal, *Musnad.* Cairo, 1311–1313/1893–1895. |
| Ibn Isḥāq | Ibn Isḥāq, *Sīrat rasūl allāh,* ed. F. Wüstenfeld. Göttingen, 1858–1859. Trans. A. Guillaume, *The Life of Muhammad.* London, 1955. |
| Ibn Sa'd | Ibn Sa'd, *Ṭabaqāt,* ed. E. Sachau. Leiden, 1905–1940. |
| IK | Ibn Kammūna |
| *JE* | *Jewish Encyclopedia.* New York and London, 1901–1906. |

| | |
|---|---|
| *Kh., Khazarī* | Yehuda Hallewi, *Kitāb al-Khazarī* (= *Das Buch al-Chazari*), ed. Hartwig Hirschfeld. Leipzig, 1887. *The Kuzari*, trans. H. Hirschfeld. New York, 1964 (orig. 1905). Trans. and abridged by Isaak Heinemann, Oxford, 1947. |
| *LHA* | R. A. Nicholson, *A Literary History of the Arabs*. Cambridge, 1907. |
| *Ma'ālim* | *Ma'ālim uṣūl al-dīn*, by Fakhr al-Dīn al-Rāzī, printed in the margin of the same author's *Muḥaṣṣal* (see below). |
| *Mabāḥit̲* | *Kitāb al-Mabāḥit̲ al-Mashriqīya*, by Fakhr al-Dīn al-Rāzī. Hyderabad, 1343/1925; Tehran, 1966. |
| *Mishkāt* | *Mishkāt al-Masabih*, tr. by James Robson. Lahore, 1963–1965. (A compilation of traditions edited by al-Baghawī, who died early in the VI/XII century, and revised by al-Khaṭīb al-Tibrizi in 737/1336. |
| *Muḥaṣṣal* | *Muḥaṣṣal afkār al-mutaqaddimīn wa-l-muta'akhkhirīn*, by Fakhr al-Dīn al-Rāzī. Cairo, 1323/1905. Cf. M. Horten, *Die Spekulative und positive Theologie des Islam. . . .* Leipzig, 1912. |
| *Munqid̲* | al-Ghazālī, *al-Munqid̲ min al-ḍalāl* (with a French trans. by F. Jabre; Collection UNESCO d'oeuvres représentatives, Série arabe). Beirut, 1959. Trans. in W. Montgomery Watt, *The Faith and Practice of Al-Ghazali*, Ethical and Religious Classics of East and West. London, 1953. Hebrew tr. by H. Lazarus-Tafeh. Tel Aviv, 1965. Cf. Vincenzo M. Poggi, S.J. *Un classico della spiritualità musulmana*. Roma, 1967. |
| *al-Najāt* | Ibn Sīnā, *al-Najāt*. Cairo, 1331/1913. |
| Noeldeke | Th. Noeldeke, *Geschichte des Qorans*. 2d ed. Leipzig, 1909–1936. |
| Samau'al | Samau'al al-Maghribī, *Ifḥām al-Yahūd: Silencing the Jews*, ed. and trans. Moshe Perlmann. |

| | |
|---|---|
| | Proceedings of the American Academy for Jewish Research, vol. 32. New York, 1964. |
| *SEI* | *Shorter Encyclopaedia of Islam.* Ithaca, 1961. |
| TB | Babylonian Talmud. |

The marginal numbers refer to the pages of the Arabic text: *Sa'd B. Manṣūr Ibn Kammūna's Examination of the Inquiries into the Three Faiths,* ed. Moshe Perlmann, University of California Publications, Near Eastern Studies no. 6. Berkeley and Los Angeles, 1967.

All page references are to original text editions.

# Introduction

VERY little is known about the author of *Examination of the Inquiries into the Three Faiths* (*Tanqīḥ al-abḥāṯ li-l-milal al-ṯalāṯ*), which was written in Arabic in Baghdad in 1280. Sa'd Ibn Manṣūr Ibn Kammūna lived from about 1215 to about 1285. He belonged to the Jewish community of Baghdad, and we also know he was probably active as a physician, possibly served as an administrator, and was mainly a teacher and writer on philosophy.

Ibn Kammuna appears to have attained a position of distinction in society and letters,[1] and a number of his works,

1. An Abū Sahl Ibn Kammūna approaches the caliph in 1121 (S. D. Goitein, in *Jewish Quarterly Review*, NS 43 [1952], 68). In a note of Aug. 11, 1967, Professor Goitein says that a Geniza fragment (TS NS J 98) mentions a poor man who bore the name Ibn Kammūna. An Ibn Kammūna died in Wāsiṭ in 1204–1205 (Ibn as-Sā'ī, *al–Jāmi' al–Mukhtaṣar*, (Baghdad, 1353–1934), p. 163, quoted by W. J. Fischel, *Jews in the Economic and Political Life of Medieval Islam*, (London, 1937, p. 136).

The chronicler Ibn al–Fuwaṭī (Fūṭī) (642–723/1244–1323) is the only substantial source of biographical data about our author.

In his biographical dictionary, *Talkhīṣ Majma' al–ādāb fī mu'jam al–alqāb*, ed. M. Jawād (Damascus, 1962), IV:1, 159–161 n. 189, Fuwaṭī mentions IK as a prominent Baghdad scholar and author, well versed in science, philosophy, letters, and especially in mathematics and logic, to whom people flocked for information. IK did not grant Fuwaṭī the interview asked for but sent him a tristich in which he warns that knowledge should be imparted only to those worthy and capable of absorbing it (cf. L. Nemoy, in *Revue des Études Juives*, Vol. 124 [1965], 507 ff.) In Fuwaṭī's chronicle *al-Ḥawādiṯ al-Jāmi'a wa-l-tajārib al-nāfi'a*, ed. M. Jawād (Baghdad, 1932), pp. 441 fn. 5, we find a comment on the attack on IK in 1284.

There is a Muslim family IK in Iraq; cf. Ḥushāwī, *Mu'jam rijāl al-fikr wa-l-'adab fī Najaf* (Najaf, 1964), pp. 380 f.

IK had the title 'Izz al-daula and his son the title Najm al-daula. The son was an official at Ḥilla and it was there that IK took refuge and died.

primarily compendia and manuals,[2] have been preserved in manuscript form.[3] References to the author's views occur in Islamic philosophical literature, and the *Examination* has been noted and quoted in Western scholarly literature for over a century. The Arabic text was published in full in 1967.[4]

The introductory note to the *Examination* explains that certain discussions on religion and religions urged the author to compile the book. Chapter I discusses the nature of prophethood and prophecy, the varieties of the prophetic experience, the criteria of its recognition, its functions, and the doubts entertained on the subject. It concludes with the statement that in the ensuing chapters an exposition of the three revelation-and-prophethood-based monotheistic religions is offered in the order of their historical emergence, with notes on the doubts and rebuttals connected with each. The three chapters that follow deal with Judaism, Christianity, and Islam. In the original the four chapters occupy 107 pages distributed as follows: chapter I, General, 20; II, Judaism, 29; III, Christianity, 16; IV, Islam, 42. Indeed, of the 87 pages on the three faiths, close to half are devoted to Islam. It shows that the author paid maximum attention to the majority faith of the Muslim lands. His ancestral faith takes second place, Christianity following as a poor third.

The *Examination* is written with studied aloofness and

---

2. D. H. Baneth, "Ibn Kammuna," in *Monatsschrift fuer Geschichte und Wissenschaft des Judentums,* 69 (1925), 295–311 n. 3, points out references in Shīrāzī (seventeenth century) and in his commentator Sabziwārī (ca. 1800); Lahijī (seventeenth century); a commentary on Maimonides.

3. *GAL,* Suppl. I, 768 f.; Suppl. III, 1232. Istanbul libraries possess several volumes of MS writings of IK (information supplied by Professor Fuat Sezgin).

L. Nemoy published Ibn Kammūna's *The Arabic Treatise on the Immortality of the Soul* (New Haven, 1945), and translated it in the *Ignaz Goldziher Memorial Volume,* Part II (Jerusalem, 1958) . Cf. Abdol Hossein Haeri, *A Catalogue of the Manuscripts in the Parliament Library,* Vol. 5 (Tehran, 1965), index.

4. See introduction to *Sa'd B. Manṣūr Ibn Kammūna's Examination of the Inquiries into the Three Faiths,* ed Moshe Perlmann, University of

objectivity, yet the fact that the book focused on Islam meant also that it contained an extensive and cumulative survey of critical remarks about Islam (with rebuttals). This led zealous Muslims to make an issue of the fact that an infidel dared to write on their faith with what they considered impudent malice and wicked design. Four years after the book was written, a mob riot against the author occurred, and he had to seek safety in flight.[5]

The sensitivity of the Muslims may have been heightened by specific circumstances. It must be borne in mind that Islam ceased to be the dominant faith after the Mongol conquest of Baghdad in 1258 (and even earlier in other areas seized by the Mongols), and that Islam had been reduced to the status of one of several religions under the rule of the pagan invaders some of whose chieftains were interested in (Nestorian) Christianity. When Ibn Kammūna wrote his *Examination* the final

---

California Publications, Near Eastern Studies no. 6 (Berkeley and Los Angeles, 1967); Fischel, *op. cit.*, pp. 134–136; Baneth's article (see n. 3, above) is the basic study on IK.

5. Fuwaṭī's account (see n. 1, above) first translated in Fischel, *op. cit.*, follows:

In this year (683/1284) it became known in Baghdad that the Jew 'Izz al-Daula Ibn Kammūna had written a volume entitled *The Inquiries on the Three Faiths,* in which he displayed impudence in the discussion of the prophecies. God keep us from repeating what he said. The infuriated mob rioted, and massed to attack his house and to kill him. The amīr Tamaskai, prefect of Iraq, Majd-al-din b. al Aṯīr, and a group of high officials rode forth to the Mustanṣirīya madrasa, and summoned the supreme judge and the [law] teachers to hold a hearing on the affair. They sought Ibn Kammūna but he was in hiding. That day happened to be a Friday. The supreme judge set out for the prayer service but, as the mob blocked him, he returned to the Mustanṣirīya. Ibn al-Aṯīr stepped out to calm the crowds, but these showered abuse upon him and accused him of being on the side of Ibn Kammūna, and of defending him. Then, upon the prefect's order, it was heralded in Baghdad that, early the following morning, outside the city wall, Ibn Kammūna would be burned. The mob subsided, and no further reference to Ibn Kammūna was made.

As for Ibn Kammūna, he was put into a leather-covered box and carried to Hilla where his son was then serving as official. There he stayed for a time until he died.

conversion of the Mongols to Islam and restoration of the dominant status of Islam were still a decade away.[6]

The book is based on excerpts: the scriptures and authoritative statements of each faith are used in the three chapters on the faiths, while the first chapter is a mosaic of reworked quotations from Jewish and Islamic philosophical-theological writings. Rarely does the author himself come to the fore, and when he does it is to act as moderator and to point out the logical acceptability or weakness of an argument adduced.

The three monotheistic faiths are based on divine revelation to and through prophets. The nature of prophetism is therefore the first inquiry and constitutes the subject of the first chapter. Following (and quoting) Avicenna (d. 1037), Ghazālī (d. 1111), Maimonides (d. 1204), and Fakhr al-Dīn al-Rāzī (d. 1209), Ibn Kammūna considers prophethood, in the light of an underlying cosmology, as a specific combination of heightened power of the psyche to absorb and emit cosmic (including psychological) influences, exceptional speculative power, and cognition of hidden verities certain enough to become a source of confidence, forceful conviction, and ability to impress and direct people toward set goals.[7] The prophet's credential is miracle-working, that is, performing acts that are extraordinary in relation to a set of conditions. The prophet's activity as it takes place in human society is a social phenomenon. Religion, cult, ritual may include seemingly irrational elements; the author adduces and discusses many doubts raised concerning faith, revelation, prophecy, and miracle.

6. Bertold Spuler, *The Muslim World* (Leiden, 1960), II, 26–36; *idem, Die Mongolen in Iran* (2d ed.; Berlin, 1955), 67–86, 178 f., 198 f.; Cl. Cahen in Kenneth M. Setton, ed., *A History of the Crusades* (Philadelphia, 1962), II, 719–725; J. A. Boyle (ed.) *The Cambridge History of Iran* (Cambridge, 1968), V, pp. 355–370.

7. F. Rahman, *Prophecy in Islam* (London, 1958); H. A. Wolfson, "Hallevi and Maimonides on Prophecy," *Jewish Quarterly Review*, n.s., 32–33 (1942), 345 ff, 349 ff; Leo Strauss, "Maimunis Lehre von der Prophetie und ihre Quellen," in *Le Monde Oriental*, 28 (1934), 99–139; L. Gardet, *Dieu et la destinée de l'homme* (Paris, 1967; Études Musulmanes Vol. IX, ed. E. Gilson and L. Gardet), sec. 2.; I. Goldziher in *Revue de Études Juives* 50 (1905), p. 32 ff.

Some readers might prefer to skip this chapter and start with the more concrete and less diffuse material in Chapter II.

Chapter II, on Judaism, is based on Yehuda Hallewi's twelfth century *Kitāb al-Khazarī*.[8] But doubtful points in and dissension on Jewish tenets are mentioned. Seven objections to Judaism are noted: (1) The base of Judaism, Jewish tradition was true, its transmission was faulty; (2) the Torah is a compilation by Ezra; (3) the Torah includes passages that cannot be of divine origin as they contain anthropomorphisms, etc.; (4) the Torah includes unworthy or worthless passages; (5) on the other hand, it does not contain such important items as the tenet of reward and punishment in a hereafter; (6) the miracle of Moses are a mainstay of Judaic belief, but why, then, should not the miracles of other claimants of prophethood be recognized; and (7) there may be abrogation of or in a divine dispensation; and, indeed, the Jews themselves practice it.

Most of these arguments are taken from a tract written in 1163–1167 by Samau'al al-Maghribī, physician-mathematician converted from Judaism to Islam.[9] Each one is followed by a rebuttal. The counterarguments are based on Hallewi at first but then increasingly on Maimonides. Samau'al is mentioned by name, but not the two Jewish authors, although Maimonides is alluded to as an eminent scholar.

In fact, as the author sees it, neither Christianity nor Islam with their dependence upon the Hebrew Scripture can afford to undermine it and its authority, hence their opposition to Judaism, and their own respective positions against it are doomed to failure. New Testament and Koran passages are cited to prove the point. The chapter closes with a remarkable sociological passage on majority-minority relations.

Chapter III, on Christianity, opens with an exposition of the faith in an excerpt from Yehuda Hallewi, followed by the Nicene creed and some comments, all amounting to one-fourth of the chapter. Twice that much space is given to the arguments of the opponents. "The best possible retort" on behalf

8. Ed. H. Hirschfeld (Leipzig, 1887).
9. Ed. M. Perlmann (New York, 1964).

of the Christians is offered next. A piece of exegesis is presented as an observation by the author (p. 64) only to be followed by rather subdued Christian arguments. The biblical passages cited here, notes the author, follow the Christian version, and not the Hebrew text. The author again expresses certain doubts. He is aware of other anti-Christian arguments but considers them unworthy. Having found that the Christians were not very effective in defending their cause, he proceeded to formulate arguments on their behalf. A tenth-century Christian theologian is mentioned, apparently from a secondhand source.

Ibn Kammūna's attitude to Jesus is reverent. Jesus, it is stressed, remained an observant Jew to the end. The same is true of many of the early Christians. Only with the apostle Paul did the new creed and sect begin to veer increasingly away from Judaism.[10]

Christianity probably did not loom large in the scope of the author's experience, despite the success of Nestorianism at the time. Christianity is made so closely dependent on Judaism that it appears to be merely a confused aberration of the latter. There seem to be inadequacies in the treatment of the subtleties of Christian theology and of the sectarian differences.

The last, largest, and decisive chapter is on Islam. It starts with a two-page summary of Islamic tenets and is followed by six arguments in favor of Islam. The first argument about Muhammad's prophethood is explored in fifteen queries and replies, which bring us to the middle of the chapter. The other five arguments and the ensuing discussion make up the second half of the chapter.

The latter draws on the works of Fakhr al-Dīn al-Rāzī, the distinguished scholar (who had died some seventy years before the *Examination* was written).[11] In this chapter the

10. This view, widely spread in Islamic literature, occurs also in Karaite writings, and indeed may have its source in early Jewish-Christian circles. Cf. Sh. Pines, *The Jewish Christians* (Jerusalem, 1966), The Israel Academy, Proceedings, II:13, pp. 42 ff.

11. On Rāzī, see G. N. Anawati in *EI*², II, 751–755 (also in A. Badawi, ed., *Ilā Ṭaha Ḥusayn* [Cairo, 1962], 193–234); Seyyed Hossein Nasr, in

excerpts are *not* always anonymous, and other Muslim authors are also referred to. It is evident that here Ibn Kammūna is addressing a public possessing a common frame of reference (which was not the case in chapters two and three), and that essentially the work was written for *Muslim* circles. Also the participation of the author comes to the fore, namely in substantial comments inserted by him as moderator and expert on logic, after the discussion of queries 3, 4, 13, 14 on argument I for Islam (pp. 74–76, 77–78, 83–84, 85). They all open with the remark 'I say.' Such comments also follow the discussion of the other Islamic arguments (pp. 90 f., 92–93, 96–98, 99–103). There is no such comment after the last argument, perhaps because the author identifies himself with the objections.

Sometimes these comments resemble passages found in Islamic compendia. They show good acquaintance with Islamic lore, literature, inner dissensions, point out the weaknesses in Islamic tradition and argumentation, and stress the role of worldly factors and interests in religious affairs, the role of *pia fraus* (p. 92).

Toward the end an anti-Islamic note may be discerned in his defense of the Jews (pp. 99–100), a defense that extends to the Christians as well (p. 101). Even the Zoroastrian permission of marriage to sisters and daughters is accepted as not rationally wrong but obnoxious to people as a result of the age-old impact of religious strictures. For that matter, even pagans are defended: idolators do not actually worship idols but seek to express their devotion to deity through their cult. On the other hand, Muhammad is seen as far from being "the most perfect man" as he appeared to the Muslims (p. 102); conversion to Islam is motivated mostly by nonreligious factors (p. 102); and Muslim argument is ultimately one of intuition, emotion, not of reason—it is essentially assertion without proof (p. 103).

It should be borne in mind that discussion of non-Islamic faiths was already quite developed in Islamic literature, wheth-

---

M. M. Sharif, ed., *A History of Muslim Philosophy* (Wiesbaden, 1963), I, 642–656; Fathalla Kholeif, *A Study on . . . Rāzī* (Beirut, 1966).

er in special treatises or in theological handbooks. If one author was unable to preserve calm, another showed an admirable measure thereof. And the same was true of polemics proper. Our author continues in the best tradition in Arabic letters.[12]

But while weighing of arguments and counterarguments was acceptable in a Muslim author, it seemed, or was made to seem, inadmissible in a non-Muslim author. Hence the success of the rabble-rouser against Ibn Kammūna. Two Muslim tracts written against the *Examination* are known by title, and a third has been preserved.[13] A Christian author wrote copious annotations on the middle chapters (on Judaism and Christianity) to vindicate his own faith.[14]

His excerpting and eclectic method notwithstanding, Ibn Kammūna stands out as an original mind in his attitude of rationality, detachment, fairness, good will, in his playing down the deceptive import of religious differences, in his stressing the humanizing and social import of religious tenets and practices, as well as in the weightiness of his skepticism. Deism bordering on agnosticism permeates the little volume, in adumbration of a mood that became prevalent—in Western literature—three or four centuries later.[15] One manifestation of

---

12. M. Steinschneider, *Polemische und apologetische Literatur in arabischer Sprache zwischen Muslimen, Christen and Juden* (Leipzig, 1877), Abhandlungen fur die Kunde des Morgenlandes VI:3; Erdmann Fritsch, *Islam und Christentum im Mittelalter* (Breslau, 1930); H. Ritter in *Der Islam*, 18 (1929).

13. A contemporary of IK, Muẓaffar al-dīn Aḥmad b. 'Alī Ibn al-Sā'ātī (d. 788/1294–1295; was he the instigator of the attack on IK?) wrote *al-Durr al-manḍūḍ fī al-radd 'alā faylasūf al-yahūd*. Zayn al-dīn Sarīja b. Muḥammad al-Malaṭī (d. 788/1386, i.e., a century after IK) wrote *Nuhūḍ ḥaṯīṯ al-nuhūḍ ilā duḥūḍ khabīṯ al-yahūd* (see Steinschneider, *op. cit.*, pp. 47 f., 107). *Kitāb iṯbāt al-nubūwa*, a tract directed against the *Examination*, has been preserved in the Süleymaniye in Istanbul.

14. M. Perlmann, "Ibn al-Maḥruma," in the *H. A. Wolfson Jubilee Volume* (Jerusalem, 1965), II, pp. 641–665.

15. "Exceptionally interesting documents of the rationalist trend in the middle ages," says Baneth (p. 295, cf. r.3) about the *Examination* and the tract about the differences between Rabbanites and Karaites. Steinschneider considered the *Examination* one of the most interesting polem-

this mood is that in the exposition, Jewish tenets (e.g., of Maimonides) are de-judaized, Islamic tenets (e.g. statements by Ghazālī, Avicenna) de-islamized in the attempt to reach the common denominator of human beliefs, attitudes, institutions.

It is possible that the chapter on Judaism shows an attempt to vindicate the faith in which the author grew up. It is certainly probable that the limited circle of Muslim intellectuals he wanted to reach was prepared for this approach, and pleased by the cool detachment of his discussion.

From Ibn Kammūna's pen we also have a treatise on the differences between the Rabbanites, the major body of Jews, and the Karaites, the minority sect that arose as a result of intellectual-spiritual fermentation (in the wake of the Islamic conquests and upheavals) in the eighth century. In its basic attitude, approach, and method this work has affinities with the *Examination.* What the latter does in the treatment of three faiths, the former does in the treatment of a rift within one faith.[16] Indeed, the author seems aware of the unusual quality of such an attitude.[17]

What stands out in Ibn Kammūna is his remarkable attempt at calm objectivity, coupled with courage and defiance, a conscious pursuit of rationality and generosity in emphasizing common humanity, and that rare attitude and quality of tolerance.

---

ical works, because it sums up the material and treats it with a remarkable objectivity that smacks of rationalism. It was to him a kind of counterpart of the untraceable *De tribus impostoribus* (*op. cit.*, pp. 37–41).

16. Printed in H. Hirschfeld's *Arabic Chrestomathy in Hebrew Characters,* (London, 1892), pp. 69–103; L. Nemoy's notes in *Tarbiz,* 24 (1955), 343–353; *idem* in *Sefer Yobel . . . for Israel Elfenbein* (Jerusalem, 1962), pp. 201–208. Nemoy has prepared a new edition as well as a translation of this tract. The text appeared in the *Proceedings of the American Academy for Jewish Research,* 36 (1968) pp. 107–165.

17. In this he calls to mind Ibn Ḥazm (e.g., in the chapter on equivalence of proofs in *Fiṣal,* V) and Ibn Khaldūn (*Muqaddima,* I, 62, Paris ed.).

In the name of the Merciful and Compassionate God. 1

I praise God for His direction and guidance. By His beatific names[1] and by His exalted attributes as revealed through His prophets and messengers, I implore Him to keep me safe in this world and in the hereafter, to place me in the eternal abode among those granted the supreme happiness, to bless those in the assembly on high and those whom He chose from mankind to be prophets and saints, and in particular His elected prophet, and the prophet's kin and companions who are endowed with supreme intellect.

Recent discussions have induced me to compose this tract as a critical inquiry into the three faiths, that is, Judaism, Christianity, and Islam. I have prefaced it with a general survey of prophethood, followed by a discussion of these religions in chronological order. Thus I began with the oldest, that is, Judaism, proceeded to the intermediate, Christianity, and concluded with the youngest, Islam. For each of these I have cited the fundamentals of its creed, without going into the particulars, as it would have been impossible to treat them all. I have followed this with an exposition of the arguments of the adherents of each faith for supporting the true prophethood of the respective founder of each. In addition, I have adduced the objections commonly raised and their rebuttals, and have drawn attention to the main issues, distinguishing the valid points from the invalid.

I have not been swayed by mere personal inclination, nor have I ventured to show preference for one faith over the other, but have pursued the investigation of each faith to its fullest extent. The tract is arranged in four chapters.

I ask God for success, guidance, a goodly end and conclusion, and that He place me in the hereafter among the believers and the pious. He distributes bounties in this world, and to Him go forth all our aspirations for eternal life. He is to be thanked for His generous favors. God is my portion and sufficiency.[2]

---

1. Cf. *EI*$^2$, I, 714 ff. God has ninety-nine such names.

2. Cf. Koran 9: 130; 39:39.

## CHAPTER 1

# *On the true nature of prophethood: its varieties, the proof of its existence, its advantages, and other matters pertaining thereto.* 2

WE find[1] that in its original condition the substance of man lacks any notion of the perceptibles beyond his immediate sensations.

At first he is endowed with the five external senses: touch, taste, smell, hearing, vision. By touch he apprehends certain existent phenomena, such as heat and cold, moisture and dryness, smoothness and roughness, and so on. With each of the other senses he apprehends other kinds of existents: tastes, odors, sounds, and colors.

Each sense fails to perceive that which the other senses perceive; nay, the perceptions of each sense are, as it were, nonexistent as far as the other senses are concerned, as for instance, colors in relation to the sense of touch, sounds in relation to the sense of smell.

When man grows beyond the world of the objects of sensations, a faculty for discernment is created in him, which is another stage of his development wherein he apprehends that which is not apparent through the external senses. This faculty he acquires as he approaches the age of seven.

Later he ascends to a third stage, that of intellect, when he apprehends notions of necessity, possibility, impossibility, and other matters not present in the stages of sensation and discernment.

Having stated this, we say that prophethood is still another stage, beyond that of intellect, in which another eye opens to

1. *Munqid*, pp. 41 f.; W. Montgomery Watt, *The Faith and Practice of Ghazālī* (London, 1953), p. 63.

see what is concealed: what will take place in the future, what has happened in the past, and other things with which intellect is as unable to cope as the power of discernment is unable to cope with the data of the intellect, and even as the senses are unable to cope with the data of discernment.

That is why we find a rationalist rejecting the data of prophethood and considering them unreasonable merely because they constitute a stage he has not attained and which is not available to him, wherefore he thinks it, *per se*, nonexistent. Similarly a man born blind, unless he has known of colors
3 and lights through hearsay and word of mouth, will not admit their existence when told about them for the first time. The same is the case of the impotent when he is told of the pleasure of sexual intercourse.[2]

Such is prophethood.[3] It has three characteristics.

The first is an inherent property within the faculty and substance of the soul which influences the material substance of the world, as well as other souls, by removing one form and creating another, and by substituting one accident for another.

The second is a property in the theoretical faculty of the prophet's soul which can become so pure as to make it thoroughly disposed for the reception of knowledge from its Bestower and Endower, with the result that intelligible objects are swiftly revealed to the prophet with no need to learn from other human beings.

The third property is that the prophet, both when asleep and awake, beholds concealed things without doubting their reality. His judgment of the truth of what he perceives is untouched by fancy or imagination, even when he perceives it in the state of sleep—in contradistinction to a person who has

---

2. The phrase occurs in Maimonides, *Introduction to Pereq Ḥeleq*, J. Kafih's edition (Jerusalem 1964) p. 203, end; also in I. Friedlaender, *Selections from the Arabic Writings of Maimonides* (Leiden, 1909), p. 15, bottom. Cf. Avicenna, *Shifā, Ilāhīyāt* II [ed. I Madkur,, Cairo, 1960] p. 424, l. 9 ff.; *Ahwal*, p. 129.

3. Based on Ghazālī, *Tahāfut*, ed. M. Bouyges (Beirut, 1962), p. 192; *idem, Maqāṣid al-falāsifa*, ed. S. Dunyā (Cairo, 1961), pp. 380–384.

veridical dreams but is uncertain of the reality of what he sees or its interpretation.

Some of the prophets possess a combination of these three gifts, others only two, and some but one, such as vision only, or a slight measure of the other qualities. The prophets are of widely differing ranks in this respect. Such is the true nature of prophethood.[4]

Prophet, or messenger, is the designation for a person who brings messages in the name of God with no human intermediary between God and himself. This includes him who is addressed by God immediately, or by a superhuman intermediary (such as an angel), or a celestial soul, or an "intelligence" in the philosophical sense, and so on.

The words "prophet" and "messenger" are sometimes applied in a more specialized sense to indicate that the person is addressed by God for the improvement of mankind. This is true in the case of a prophet sent with a comprehensive religion, but not every prophet is of this kind. Some prophets have been sent, for instance, to announce the chastisement of a
people or a person, or to announce a matter that will occur 4
in the future, or has occurred in the past, as is told about many a prophet of the Israelites after Moses. These followed the Mosaic faith, and were not sent to launch a faith of their own; rather they were sent on particular missions that affected all or some of the people of their times.[5]

Among those who recognize the existence of prophethood there are three different points of view.[6]

The first view is held by those who say that God chooses for prophethood whom He wishes, and it makes no difference whether that person is learned or ignorant, old or young, but they posit the condition that the person possess a certain excellence and be morally fit—for no one goes so far as to assert

4. *Guide*, Book II, chap. 36; cf. also p. 93*a* (ch. 45).

5. Islamic theology distinguishes between the call to prophethood and the command to preach; also between prophethood within a faith, and the mission to establish a new faith.

6. *Guide*, Book II, chap. 32, pp. 72*b* ff.

that God would send a wicked man as prophet without first turning him into a good man.

The second view is that prophethood is a certain perfection in the nature of man, attained only after a training that makes what is potential in the species pass into the actual, except where prevented by a constitutional defect or external cause. Those who hold this view maintain that only a superior person of perfect rational and moral qualities will become a prophet, and that whoever is fit for prophethood and has prepared for it must necessarily become a prophet.

The third view is held by those who consider that prophethood is attained only by a superior and perfect person, yet believe that, although fit for prophethood and prepared for it, one may, by God's will and decree, not become a prophet.

Such are the views known to us on this subject.

A prophet[7] may receive a measure of inspiration that will affect him alone and render him perfect, or he may receive so much that it compels him to call upon the people in order to teach them and let his perfection emanate unto them. Similarly, in the case of scientists, one may feel neither the urge nor the ability to teach others or compose works, while another is moved of necessity to compose works and to teach. Were it not for the latter compulsion, the sciences would not be set forth in books, nor would prophets call upon the people to obtain knowledge of the truth. This is embedded in the nature of men of science and of prophets, just as the sexual drive is embedded in the nature of man and of other animals for procreation, by the providence of God for His creatures
5 (Glory unto Him!). The scientist as well as the prophet sometimes feels an internal drive to direct people toward their good and to call people toward good, irrespective of whether the people are receptive.

Prophetic inspiration is divided rationally into four categories, for it may come (1) in dream, (2) in the state of waking, and in each case either (3) through the medium of an angel

7. *Ibid.*, chap. 37, p. 81*a*.

or other being, or (4) possibly without a medium.[8] The prophet, when making his public appeal, may or may not disclose which of these categories applies to him.

A prophet may prophesy in parables because his vision comes to him in that form. The meaning of the parable may be explained to him during his vision, as when, for instance, a man sees a dream and imagines therein that he awakes, relates the dream to another person, and explains its meaning to him, yet all of this takes place within the dream.

The meanings of some prophetic parables are not interpreted during the vision, but the prophet subsequently learns of their intent by divine inspiration. In such parables the prophet sees something, the name of which may indicate its meaning to him by way of derivation or homonymity, so that one meaning might lead to another. This, too, is a kind of parable-making and it is attributed to some Hebrew prophets.

The indication[9] may occur through a noun whose letters are, in a different order, those of another noun, even though there is no relation between the two words in either derivation or homonymity. Just as a man may see in his dream that he has departed for a certain land, married there, stayed there for a time, that a son was born to him whom he called a certain name, and that such and such things happened to the son, so the like may appear in prophetic parables, even when lengthy intervals of time between one action and another are mentioned, in the manner of a parable. In prophetic speech, metaphors and figurative expressions, as well as expressions of hyperbole, often occur;[10] thus, he who accepts such words in their original sense may be utterly mistaken.

Saintliness[11] borders on the rank of prophethood. Not 6
every saint is considered a prophet, but every prophet is a saint. A saint bordering on the prophetic rank may enjoy divine assistance that moves and encourages him to a major

8. *Ibid.*, chap. 43.
9. *Ibid.*, chaps. 43, 46, pp. 91*a–b*.
10. *Ibid.*, chap. 46, p. 97*b*.
11. *Ibid.*, chap. 45, pp. 93*b*–94*a*.

righteous action of great impact, such as the deliverance of a virtuous community from a community of the wicked, or the deliverance of a great and virtuous person, or the radiation of good upon a multitude of people. He feels in himself a drive, an urge to act. A divine spirit rests upon such a person, not to make him speak but to move him to action, and not any chance action, but a particular action that succors or leads to the deliverance of a wronged one, be it a single great man or a community. Just as not everyone who has had a veridical dream is a prophet, so, also, it is not to be said about everyone who has enjoyed divine help in some chance matter, such as acquisition of wealth or fulfillment of personal ambition, that a divine spirit has settled upon him, or that he is a saint, or that he has acted through the Holy Spirit. That may be said only of him who has performed a righteous act of great impact or an action that led to such a righteous act.

A saint[12] may feel that something has descended upon him, that an outside force has overtaken him, making him speak. He then speaks in wise maxims, or praise of God, or beneficial locutions of admonition, or in normative commands of divine origin—all in the state of waking, with the habitual possession of his senses. Of such a person is it said that the Holy Spirit speaks through him.

These two stages of saintliness are below the stage of genuine prophethood. The stages and stations of sainthood are numerous, and discussing them is beyond the purpose of this book; these two stations have been mentioned here only in order to pass from them to a discussion of the degrees of genuine prophethood.

Of these I will mention ten.

In the first degree the prophet sees a parable in a dream, according to the conditions concerning prophethood mentioned above, and in that very parable clearly perceives its meaning and intent.

In the second degree he hears clear, distinct speech in a dream without seeing the speaker.

---

12. *Ibid.*, p. 94*a*.

In the third degree a human being addresses him in a dream.

In the fourth degree an angel addresses him in a dream.

In the fifth degree he sees God, as it were, addressing him in a dream.

In the sixth degree a revelation in the form of a parable comes to him while he is awake.

In the seventh degree he hears speech while awake.

In the eighth degree it is as if a human being were addressing the prophet in his waking state.

In the ninth degree he sees, while awake, an angel addressing him.

In the tenth degree he sees, while awake, that God is addressing him.[13] 7

These are the reported degrees of prophethood.[14]

A prophet[15] may experience one degree of revelation at one time, and a different—higher or lower—degree at another time. It may be that he will reach the high degree only once in his life, or even attain prophethood only once in his life-

---

13. The degrees of prophethood:

| In Maimonides | In Ibn Kammūna |
|---|---|
| 1. Divine assistance<br>2. The prophet is urged to speak in public | Sainthood of *auliyā'* |
| 3. Parable clearly perceived in dream | 1. Same |
| 4. Speech heard in dream | 2. " |
| 5. Human speaker heard in a dream | 3. " |
| 6. Angel heard in a dream | 4. " |
| 7. As if God heard in a dream | 5. " |
| 8. Parable in vision (not dream) | 6. Parable in waking state (*yaqẓa*) |
| 9. Speech heard in vision | 7. Same |
| 10. Human speaker heard in vision | 8. " |
| 11. Angel heard in vision | 9. " |
| 12. God heard in waking state | 10. " |

In Maimonides the last degree is reserved for one prophet only, namely Moses. Ibn Kammūna omits mentioning Moses, thereby dejudaizing the scale.

14. *Guide*, Book II, chap. 45.

15. *Ibid.*, opening at chap. 45.

time. Prophethood may be cut off from him, and he may grieve over it and yearn for it. Revelation may come to him in a disturbing manner, as hearing speech that is like mighty thunder, or seeing terrible, awesome pictures. The possibilities are almost infinite. Examples of them have been reported about the Hebrew prophets, peace upon them, and can be found in the books of their prophecies.

Miracles are one of the indications of the veracity of those who lay claim to prophethood.[16]

A miracle, by definition, is that which humans are unable to perform or attain because of a lack of power or knowledge or instrument. Most believers take it for granted that a miracle is proof that justifies the prophet's claim to prophethood.

[The believers] stipulate many conditions that must be met for a miracle to serve as proof of prophethood. One is that other humans cannot perform the act or anything approaching it. Another is that it be contrary to the customary course [of nature]. Further, that it should occur at the time it is promulgated, that it take place at the time the prophet claims prophethood, and that it be of God's doing or by His command and with His help. These are the five conditions.

Our condition that other people be unable to perform the miracle is laid down because that which men are able to do is common to the truthful man and to the liar. If their claims are comparable, the truthful one will be indistinguishable from the other. The same holds true in the case of something approximating a miracle, for on rare occasions there may be a man of learning or an expert in a craft who surpasses his contemporaries and others in performance, yet this is not necessarily an indication of prophethood, even if we posit that he
8 has issued a challenge [to contest him]. But it would be proof of prophethood if he attained such a degree of excellence as would lead to the conclusion that what he had performed, or even approximated, was beyond human capacity.

We further stipulated that the miracle must be contrary

---

16. *Ma‘ālim*, margins of pp. 97 f.; *Arba‘īn*, p. 316, bottom.

to the customary course [of nature] because only this proves the truth of the claim, so that, were it not for the truth of the claim, the phenomenon would not occur. It is impossible to say, "were this prophet not in the right, the sun would not rise today," for it rose today for the same reason that it did yesterday.

We stipulated that the miracle occur at the time it is promulgated, for it has been argued that if a different time is set, causes unrelated to the truth of the prophetic claim may intervene to disrupt the customary course [of nature].

We stipulated that the miracle happen in the course of claiming prophethood because the rightness of the claim is an attribute of the claim, and the attribute cannot exist without that to which it is attributed.

We stipulated that it must be a deed performed by God or with His permission, because confirmation of a claim is proof of the truth of the claim only if he who confirms or urges or enables confirmation is wise. Reasonable people see no difference between 1) A giving his seal to B who will declare it to be a sign and proof of being the messenger of A, and 2) enabling B to take the seal knowing it supports his claim to being A's messenger. That is why the acts of verification and enabling are equivalent in proving the truth.

If these conditions converge, we know that the disruption of the natural course of events is connected with the claim to prophethood and occurred for the sake of the prophet, and it will serve as verification of the claim. It is as if a man said to another, "If I am your messenger, put your hand on your head"; if the other acts thereupon, he would be saying thereby: you are right in your claim to being a messenger. If the miracle served as the verification for a claimant to prophethood, and God presumably cannot grant verification to a man who speaks falsely, it would be established that the claimant was right.

Seven doubts have been raised concerning this point.[17]

---

17. The objections echo older sources, such as Ibn al-Rāwandī and Muḥammad Ibn Zakaryā al-Rāzī (IX. cent.).

22

First: Disruption of natural order is impossible. Admitting disruption in nature leads to sophistry, for if we admit such disruption, we are not sure that mountains would not turn to gold, and seas flow with blood, and when we saw an old man we would have to admit that he may just have come into existence, without father and mother. And if we saw Zayd, it would be possible that he was another person whom God had created in the same fashion and physique. All of which is nonsense.

Second: Why do you say that this miracle has been accomplished by divine origination, or command, or capacita-
9 tion? Possibly the prophet's soul is different from other souls, or his constitution or composition is different from that of other human beings, and it is this specific quality that is the source of that specific power; or it may be that he has found a drug that has the power to bring about these results; or that jinn, devils, or some celestial force assisted him in an act performed as a piece of disobedience toward God.

Third: We do not concede that God created the miracle to verify [prophethood] for His acts are above [specific] purposes.

Fourth: If we should concede that God acts for a purpose, why do you say that in creating the miracle He had no purpose but to verify [a prophetic claim]? Perhaps it is the beginning of a [new] natural phenomenon like the beginnings of other chains of phenomena? Or it is some recurrent phenomenon that appears only at protracted intervals which human life-span is insufficient to determine. Or it may occur so that the faithful should be wary and not regard it as proof of verification of a prophetic claim, despite the difficulty of such reserve, in which event he may be rewarded for this reserve. It is said that this applies to the interpretation of the ambiguous [scripture] verses. Again, the miracle may occur for some purpose we do not fathom, as it is beyond human power to fathom all of God's wisdom.

Fifth: If all things are of God's creation, it is He who creates the sinner's depravity and the infidel's godlessness. If that be so, the creation of a godlessness-inspiring miracle is not more far-fetched than the creation of godlessness itself. If that be so, divine verification for the prophet is no proof of the prophet's being right in substance.

Sixth: When one person says to another, "If I am your messenger, do such and such," and the second does it, we refuse to accept this as a proof of verification. For it is possible that an independent cause made that man produce that act at that time.

Seventh: Even if we granted that the person [addressed] had no other purpose than to confirm the claims of the speaker, we would not grant that this was proof of divine confirmation of the prophet's performance of a miracle which disrupts [the course of nature], because while we know well the circumstances of that person, his character, his manners of action, and while we might surely know that he acted as he did only to produce verification, nobody [can] know and fathom God's procedure with His deeds and creatures. Indeed, can His acts be compared to those of humans?

In reply to the first doubt it is maintained that a general admission of the possibility of a phenomenon does not preclude the assertion that the phenomenon did not occur at a specific time. So that even if we admit the creation of a pseudo-Zayd, or the creation of a man without parents, it does not contradict our assertion that this Zayd is the one whom we have known, and that this [particular] old man was born to parents, was first a child and then aged until he became an old man. This is self-evident knowledge which God created for man, lest the order of reality deteriorate by nonrecognition and doubt concerning the normal course of events.[18]

In reply to the second doubt, it has been said that there is no originator but God, and that if this be admitted, then, as we explained, to make origination possible is equivalent to origination. The All-Wise will not tolerate such deviation lest it lead to religious error.

In reply to doubt number three: [The very] creation of a miracle points to verification of God Himself. By its very na-

18. *Muḥaṣṣal*, p. 156; *Ma'ālim*, p. 104. *Arba'īn*, p. 316.

ture, miracle involves divine verification. Even if this be called a [specific] purpose, why should this interpretation be considered absurd?

In reply to doubt number four: Immediate knowledge is created in us that the miracle is designed to verify [the claim of prophethood] and not to bear out other possibilities.

The other doubts may be answered similarly. Once the existence of a thing is known as evident, allowing the opposite possibility does not discredit this evident knowledge.

The difference between the miracles of the prophets and the wonders worked by saints is that those of the latter type, unlike those of the former, are not coupled with the claim to prophethood.

The difference between miracles and sorcery—among those who admit of the latter—is that the sorcerer, should he falsely claim prophethood, would either be opposed by a divinely ordained person, or he would not be able to perform the sorcery he formerly was able to perform.

Foolish people may confuse a miracle with other unusual phenomena or illusions—for example, with those displayed by jugglers and masters of natural and mechanical tricks. A sensible person should beware of this error, for many have been misled.

Philosophers say that the images of angels and others seen by prophets, even when the prophets say "we see God," are like the veridical dreams seen by other people in sleep. But the difference is one of intensity. In the case of the prophets, as explained above, the power of the vision reaches the stage of certainty beyond doubt, which is not true of the other dreamers.

[The philosophers] say that generated things follow only
11 from their causes, and the knowledge of the full cause entails the knowledge of the effect of that cause. Generated things may be grasped before they come into existence, not insofar as they are possible, but insofar as they are necessitated [by their causes]. If some factors of a thing are clear to us while others remain unknown, then to the extent that they are clear to us, we have an idea of the actual existence [of those gen-

erated things]; and insofar as some factors remain unknown, we begin to doubt their actual existence. The disposition of the world for what is to occur is imprinted in the supernal principles. Those principles are either celestial souls, or their bodies [spheres], or abstract intellects. These souls or intellects are the equivalent, in philosophical terminology, of the angels. Those principles in turn are not *per se* inaccessible to our souls at all, but are veiled because our faculties either are weak or are not applied in a direction by which one can attain these principles. If neither of these [defects] is in evidence, union with the principles will be achieved and a measure of the hidden attained by our powers. [This knowledge] then progresses to the imagination, where the imaginative faculty with its mobile imitative capacity passes from one thing or person to another, leaving what it caught, evoking its like or opposite or counterpart—just as a person who is awake may observe something, be led by imagination to other things, forget the first thing, and not return to it except after some analysis and conjecture. On the other hand, the imaginative faculty may not pass on but will stay at what it has captured, and the matter may rest without further transference. Veridical vision, if of this kind, needs no interpretation.[19]

The imaginative faculty may reach a stage of such perfection that sensory faculties will not congest it with their communications and thus will not prevent it from helping the rational soul to get in contact with those principles with which it is inspired. Then the rational soul may receive the image of the unknown in the waking state, and further, the imaginative force may act as it does in a state of vision that needs interpretation. Sometimes wondrous divine images are witnessed, coupled with audible divine voices, which are like those revealed apprehensions. Still stronger is the case when these situations and images persist without the imaginative faculty imitating them. As for the imaginative faculty, sensation may preoccupy it with whatever perceptible forms reach

---

19. The paragraph is based on Ibn-Sīnā. *Ahwal*, pp. 116–117.

it, and sometimes the intellect preoccupies it, deflecting it from imagining falsehoods, which are neither induced by sense perception nor operated by the intellect. The convergence of these two distractions may prevent the imaginative force from completing its appropriate actions.

If either of the two distractions is eliminated, it is possible
that the imaginative faculty will resist the remaining one;
however that remaining impediment will still exercise an
12 effect. Sometimes the imaginative faculty becomes free of the
attraction of the senses, and is strong enough to resist the
intellect, as in the state of sleep when the imaginative faculty
brings forth images as something seen. Sometimes the imaginative faculty becomes free of the rule of reason when the
mechanism employed by reason in regulating the body goes
awry; the imaginative faculty then overrides sense, does not
allow it to interfere, and proceeds to accomplish its own actions. Then the images it initiates also become like things
seen, as in the case of sickness, strong fear, and insanity. That
is why in the insane and the abnormal, as a result of their
strong rejection of the senses, especially in cases of epilepsy
and fainting, the functions of their sensory forces are impaired;
and while their minds are deflected from what the senses perceive, they may see hidden things. This in turn may lead to
imagining things, and these will be like things seen and heard.
If an abnormal person announces a hidden matter and the out-
come is then in accordance with what he says, that is sooth-
saying. It occurs because of his defectiveness. But in the case
of the prophets, [the similar result is stronger owing to] their
great perfection. As their contact with the higher principles
is stronger, and their perceptions are more complete, they are
consciously certain of perceiving hidden things without any
doubt about their findings, whether attained in the waking
state or in sleep. If they do not attain certainty about their
findings, their perception is not prophetic, even if they have
attained prophethood on a previous occasion. Such then is the
secret of their knowledge of the hidden and their perception
of forms.

As to the perfection of the prophets' speculative intellect.[20] the syllogism's middle term, which must be perceived in order to understand unknown intelligibles, is sometimes attained by intuition, and sometimes by instruction, but the origins of learning are intuitive. Things certainly can be traced to the intuitions of masters who then conveyed them to their disciples. Intuition may occur to a man within himself, and the syllogism may be concluded in his mind without a teacher. There are variations in this matter. Some people will intuit a greater number of middle terms; others will intuit them more rapidly. At one extreme is a person without intuition, at the other, one who has a rich intuition—on all or most subjects—or one who is granted the most rapid intuition. There may exist a person so favored by intense purity and so firmly linked to the high principles that he will use intuition in everything that is within human power to grasp—or in most things, or in many things, even if not most—and he will learn those things not through the uncertain method of learning from a teacher but by arriving at the middle term of apodictic syllogisms.

As to the secret of the prophets' miraculous deeds: the world's matter submits to the impact of the forms arising in the souls and intelligences in the spiritual world. The intelligible forms among them are the source for the sensory forms, 13
a source from which are derived the varieties of the species known in the bodily world. The human soul is purely spiritual. It is similar to the substance of heavenly spiritual beings. The matter of the soul's body submits to the soul just as matter throughout the world submits to those higher spiritual substances.

A man may possess a soul whose influence transcends his body; and, if his soul wishes, it produces in the world of matter that which it imagines. Then movement and repose, heating and cooling, and so on, will take place in matter as they do in that man's body and as his soul produces them in his body. That will be followed by the formation of clouds and winds,

---

20. *al-Najāt*, pp. 272 f.; *De Anima*, pp. 248 ff. *Ahwal*, p. 122 f. The preceding paragraph is based on *Ahwal*, p. 120 f.

storms, quakes, bursting forth of waters, wells, and so on, by virtue of the will of that man.

The most perfect of mankind is he who, when related to the world of intellect, seems to be fully part of it, and, when related to the world of soul, seems to be one of its dwellers, and, when related to the world of nature, acts therein at will.

He who reaches this stage is necessarily perfect in character, noble, of pure soul, and bent on good deeds. He attains the highest ranks of the prophets, and reaches perfect human happiness and ceaseless bliss.

Know that not every essence that we imagine necessarily exists.

Now that we have explained what prophethood is, its division and symptomatic miracles, and its causes, how the prophet hears the speech of God and sees His angels, and how they take on visible shape, we must prove the existence of the prophet and the ultimate reason therefor. We shall speak of this as philosophers have taught it.

We say[21] that man is distinguished from other living beings by the fact that he cannot enjoy a good life as long as he is left to himself in the conduct of his affairs, and is without the cooperation of others of his species in obtaining the necessities of life, so that, for example, one acts as green-grocer, another as baker, another as tailor, another as needle-maker. Cooperation is impossible without mutual contact, which must have some pattern and just measure. This presupposes someone who sets the pattern and the just measure, and it must be a human being who addresses men and makes them adhere to what he has set. If men were left to their own views there would be discord.

14 He who carefully considers God's providence for His creation finds that such a person is more necessary for the welfare of mankind than many things whose supply has not been neglected by divine providence, such as the growth of hair for

21. Adapts Avicenna, *Shifā', Ilāhiyāt* (Cairo, 1960), pp. 441–446; *al-Najāt*, pp. 498 f.; *Mabāḥiṯ*, II, 523. Cf. A. J. Arberry, *Avicenna on Theology* (London, 1951), p. 42; also *Guide*, Book II, chap. 40. *Greengrocer* (*yabqul*) following the *Shifā'* text, not *conveyor* (*yanqul*).

the eyelashes and eyebrows, the arch in the sole of the foot, and such other advantages as are not necessary to survival, yet are useful to some extent. If divine providence supplied those lesser benefits, how then should it not provide the more important? It is impossible that the First Principle, and after it the Angels, should be aware of one and not of the other, for divine knowledge embraces everything. If God knows what is necessary in order to attain the good, then that certainly must exist. If that which depends on the existence of the prophet exists, then certainly he must exist.

It is evident that this man, the legislator (= founder of religion), should be distinguished in some way from all other men, or else he would be no different from any other person; acceptance of his instruction would not be more binding than the acceptance of any other tenets, and discord would disrupt legislation itself. What distinguishes him are the miracles, announced by him, and proving the certainty of his mission, as mentioned above.

Know that sheer benefit [to mankind] is not sufficient to confirm the existence of a prophet. For this benefit is present when a man is believed by reason of his magic or the power of suggestion to be a prophet, even if he is no prophet at all, as we find it in the social structure in many pagan polities. Rather, additional merits must be present which we shall mention, and which are characteristic only of true prophethood. Belief may become entrenched in the soul not by a certain recorded proof, but by causes, concomitants, and experiences whose details are without number. Veridical dreams are, as it were, a pattern of prophecy. Sometimes sufficient intuition results for belief in the source of prophethood. Or else certainty therein is attained by witnessing or listening, or from communication with another. If you know medicine, for example, you know that so-and-so is a physician because of what you hear about him and what you see of his works. You likewise believe in the existence of prophethood after you know its essence and true nature.

The fundamental principle in the true prophet's legislation is to teach people that they have One Creator, Living,

Almighty, who has no companion to share His rule, who is peerless, who knows the secret and the manifest, and from whose knowledge nothing is hidden upon earth or in the heavens, who is rightly to be obeyed, and who has prepared bliss for him who obeys, and wretchedness for him who disobeys; and that he, the prophet, should establish among men the principle of life hereafter, the existence of pleasure eternal that is a great possession, and of suffering that is an everlasting chastisement.

Inasmuch as such a prophet is of a kind whose existence will recur but infrequently, since matter susceptible of such perfection occurs in but a few temperaments, it is necessary that he should enjoin the people to perform repeatedly, at short intervals, acts and deeds that he has stipulated for them. These should be linked to a reminder about God and the life hereafter, lest they be forgotten within a generation or even later. Those facts and deeds are the rites of worship—such as prayers, fasts, pilgrimages, holy wars, sacrifices, alms-giving and the like: acts or the abandonment of acts, as ordered by the prophet, and by which men benefit in this world and in the life hereafter.

Among these acts of worship there may be some whose benefit cannot be fathomed by reason. One should neither avoid nor reject them. In the stipulations of religious law there may be special properties for treating and purifying the heart that cannot be grasped by rational philosophy, nay, will be discerned only in the prophetic phase, as mentioned earlier. Similarly,[22] the negative injunctions in religious law may refer to harmful things understandable [as such] only in that phase. In a similar vein is the case of the specific properties of drugs and poisons, and, if what is said be true, of the influence of talismans. Then too, were it not for our observation that man is formed in cohabitation, in the womb, feeding upon menstrual blood, we should deny that the existence of such a noble life is the result of such a base and impure act. Possibly analogous is the case of sacrifices and the like in religious

22. *Munqiḏ*, pp. 51 f.

precepts, whose benefits in this world and in the hereafter are not apparent to us, apart from the sheer reward [promised for] performing them.

Fifteen benefits have been quoted that are inherent in the sending of prophets and messengers.[23]

*The first* is that we are taught what rites of worship are desired from us, in substance and quantity. For even if we rationally admit that in principle we owe obedience to God, we 16
still do not know how to be obedient. God then sends his messengers to resolve this difficulty.

*The second* is that inadvertence and negligence are parts of man's nature, and caprice and passions have power over him. The sending of prophets is of help to him: they alert man to inadvertence, and prevent the rule of caprice over him. If man were left to himself, his caprice, he would be exposed to the lure of those evils.

*The third* is that even if we know rationally how good are belief and the practice of righteous deeds, and how evil are unbelief and the practice of repugnant deeds, still we do not know rationally that positive behavior deserves eternal and abundant reward while negative behavior deserves great punishment in the hereafter—especially since we know that the repugnant deed may give us transitory pleasure and there is no harm in it for God. The sending of prophets obviates these difficulties.

*The fourth* is that we know rationally only those attributes of God of which we learn through His acts, while of His other attributes we can learn only through the report of prophecy.

*The fifth* is that, were it not for God sending prophets, man might remain afraid and say: if I concentrate on obedience, I may still act in God's realm not in accordance with His wish, but if I do not—I may be chastised for failing in obedience. Man will then be fearful in both cases. With prophecy, his fear ceases.

---

23. *Muḥaṣṣal*, p. 156.

*The sixth* is that a thing may be repugnant to us when it is not repugnant in itself. Prophecy will distinguish between the two cases.

*The seventh* is that, of things created in this world of generation and corruption, some may be nutriments, some remedy, or some poison; and only after long periods does experience prove sufficient to distinguish them, even when their action is mostly dangerous. In prophecy, there is the benefit of how, without harm or danger, to know and use things. This has been used as an argument for the existence of prophethood; that is, the existence of prophethood is argued from the fact that there exists in the world some knowledge whose rational acquisition cannot be imagined, for example, the knowledge of medicine. He who has studied the properties of drugs, simple and compound, inevitably recognizes that they can be grasped only by divine inspiration and divine instruction. We thus conclude that there is a nonrational way to grasp such matters and that they have been grasped in a different phase, one that is above reason, namely the phase of prophecy.

17 *The eighth* is that some astronomical phenomena recur only at great intervals. But while in experience recurrence is basic, human life spans will not suffice to establish the cycles of the planets. Thus, astronomical instruments are insufficient to supply knowledge about Mercury because it is small, concealed, has little light, and is constantly close to the sun, both when rising and setting; and so with other data of this science.

*The ninth* is the proper guidance in the beneficial crafts which cannot be gained by mere reason, and which each person learns from another. They were originally taught by means of prophecy, by revelation, or inspiration.

*The tenth* is that for the good life, the knowledge of ethics, home management, and public governance is indispensable; and prophecy must exist in order to teach it.

*The eleventh* is that man is by nature social, and interdependence may give rise to rivalry, which may lead to lethal fighting. A law must be imposed by a legislator, that is, the prophet.

*The twelfth* is that if the shaping of legislation were

delegated to people, then perhaps each group would produce a different specific scheme and even the people of a particular polity would hardly agree on law, which might lead to discord. Laying down a single law for the community (*umma*) counteracts this danger.

*The thirteenth* is that what man does by virtue of reason is akin to a habitual act, but habit is not worship. Yet whatever is enjoined by one who is greatly revered will be performed out of pure worship, even when man does not grasp the reason for the injunction. This is perhaps one of the benefits in the command to perform strange acts of worship.

*The fourteenth* is that minds are different, perfect beings rare, divine mysteries precious, and the sending of prophets as well as the revelation of scriptures is necessary so that everyone may be prepared to proceed toward the utmost perfection possible for him, each in accordance with his personality.

*The fifteenth* is that in every genus are species, one of which is perfect. The same relationship exists between the species and the family, between the family and the individual, and between the individual and the limbs. The noblest of limbs, their chief, is the heart; and its vice-regent is the brain. From the heart, forces run throughout the parts of the body. Similarly, man must have a chief. The chief must either rule only the outward aspect, which is [done by] the ruler (*sulṭān*), or
only the inward aspect, which is [done by] the learned (*ʿālim*), 18
or must rule both, and that is [done by] the prophet or by him who occupies the prophet's place in his time or after him. Thus the prophet is like the heart, and the learned man comes next like the brain. Just as the perceptive powers emanate from the brain to the limbs, so the powers of interpretation and instruction emanate through the "vice-regent" unto all men of knowledge.

This is what has been mentioned of the advantages accruing from the prophetic mission. Some of it depends on persuasion, not certainty.

Those who deny prophecy have three doubts.[24]

24. *Arbaʿīn,* pp. 324 ff.; *Muḥaṣṣal,* p. 154. In Islamic texts such views are usually ascribed to the Barāhima of India; cf. *EI*$^2$s.v.

34

*The first* is that the purpose of sending prophets is to make people responsible (*taklīf*). But the suggestion [of human responsibility] is erroneous, and consequently [the notion of] sending prophets is erroneous. We say this for six reasons.

First is that, were man actually charged with performing or relinquishing a certain deed, then, if he opts for performing but is not free to relinquish it, he is forced to perform the deed; he has no choice between relinquishment and performance, and thus in no way will he have free choice and responsibility. If he is free to relinquish the deed, then he must decide between two courses and prefer one over the other, as there is no distinction of one of two equals without a specifier. That specifier, if it be a human act, still goes back ultimately to an act of God, not to human acts. If the act occurs, and yet it is possible that it should not occur, then sometimes it will occur, and sometimes it will not, and the chances for either course are equal. Then again, disinction is without specifier. If it is impossible for the preferred act not to occur, then when it happens, it is inevitable; and when an act does not occur, it is because it is impossible for it to occur, so that man is neither choosing, nor responsible.

Second is that God is omniscient. If, therefore, man is made responsible for a certain thing that must occur, then his responsibility for it is absurd; if, however, its nonoccurrence is known and it is impossible for the thing to occur, the imposition of responsibility for it would then be iniquitous. Furthermore, the benefit of responsibility is reward; but, if the existence of the reward is known, there is no need for the act of obedience, and if the nonexistence of reward is known—there is no sense in the act of obedience.

Third. In the case of equal urges—to act and to desist—*taklīf* is absurd because preferring is impossible without a preferrer. In case one of the urges prevails, the discarded alternative is [something] impossible, because [only] if it is impossible is the equality of alternative eliminated. It is proper
19 that as a discarded alternative it be impossible, but when the discarded alternative is impossible, the prevailing one is surely

[something] necessary. Thus *taklīf* is pointless both in the case of the necessary and of the impossible.[25]

Fourth. Imposing a responsibility makes no sense. If it occurred it would be absurd. Nor would it befit the Divine Wisdom. Proof thereof is that if *taklīf* made sense it would either depend on him who imposes responsibility, that is God, or on some other (force). But God is above benefit or harm, gain or loss, while man's benefits are confined to pleasure and joy, the elimination of pain and grief, and whatever is conducive thereto. Deity can grant all this to man without the medium of imposed responsibility.

Fifth. The imposition of responsibility for his acts upon one who is destined to disbelief and sin is unbefitting the Divine Wisdom. Because if the imposed obligation is fulfilled, it would mean that the Deity is ignorant (God is utterly above such notions); and if the obligation is not fulfilled, man deserves punishment. No act leading to either of the reprehensible alternatives can issue from God Most Merciful and Most Wise.[26]

---

25. *Arbaʿīn,* p. 234, bottom.

A thing is either necessary and will occur, or impossible and will not occur. Equal chance really does not exist: as long as not all the factors are known there may be a semblance of equal chance. *Taklīf* may mean imposing the necessary or the impossible. The necessary will occur irrespective of *taklīf*; the impossible will not occur irrespective of *taklīf*.

What then is the sense of *taklīf*, of human responsibility?

S. Horovitz (cf. n. 26) refers to Plutarch *De Stoic. Repugn.*, ch. 23. Plutarch reports that certain philosophers maintained that sometimes the soul shows the presence of an incidental power (*epeleustikē dȳnamis/kīnēsis*) "For then, with two things altogether alike and of equal importance, there is a necessity to choose the one, there being no cause inclining to either, for that neither of them differs from the other. This adventitious power of the soul, seizing on its inclination, determines the doubt." Chrysippus (280–209 B.C.) opposed this theory as negating causality, and suggested that, e.g. in the case of equal chance (in dice or the movement of the balance), some concealed, obscure, but real, causes (*aitiai adēloi*) are acting and bring upon the result that one side prevails.

26. Cf. ʿAbd al-Jabbār al-Asadābādī (d. 415/1025; cf. *EI²*), *al-Mughnī* (Cairo, 1965), XI, pp. 129, 138, bottom, 139, l. 5, 159, 164 ff., 224, 293 ff.,

Sixth. The acts imposed upon man deflect him from devoting himself to the knowledge of God and love for Him. But it is man's most pressing duty to forego everything that hinders him therefrom.

In reply to all this, it has been said that the imposition of responsibility implies letting man know that he who has done the commendable deed will have therein a sign of a reward to come; while he who has not done so will have a sign of impending punishment. Nobody can question God's destining one man for reward and another for punishment, for just as His essence is not motivated, so neither are His deeds.

*The second* doubt concerns a prophet's message. If its substance is rationally recognized as good, it is welcome irrespective of whether a prophet revealed it or not. Then prophecy is superfluous. If the message is rationally recognized as evil, it is to be rejected rationally. If neither its goodness nor its evil is evident, then, if it answers a need, it is put to the test and may prove useful (the imposition of the humanly impossible does not befit divine wisdom), but if there is no need for it, we reject it to avoid possible harm.[27]

The reply is that the purpose of the mission of prophets is to teach that which cannot be grasped by mere reason.

*The third* doubt. In (religious) law we see acts prescribed which are unbefitting wisdom, such as strange rites in the pilgrimage; excessive prayer, fasting, going on pilgrimage are of no use to the Deity, and are burdensome and tiresome for man. Some of these acts cause the rationalists to scoff at those who perform them. How could it befit the Most Wise to send messengers to have these acts performed? Among other things, the prophets clarified certain dubious points, such as specifying a certain house for worship in preference to other

---

511, 517. Cf. R. Brunschwig, "Devoir et Pouvoir," *Studia Islamica,* XX (1964); S. Horovitz in the German Oriental Society's Journal v. 57 (1903), note on p. 190.

27. 'Abd al-Jabbār, *op. cit.,* p. 563, bottom. The argument was voiced by Ibn al-Rāwandī, and reproduced by many authors. Cf. P. Kraus, "Beitraege zur islamischen Ketzergeschichte," *Rivista degli studi orientali,* XIV (1934), 97, 111 n. 3, 344 f., 347 n. 2.

houses, or specifying the time for certain rituals, though other periods might serve equally well. There are many such points in the religious codes.

The answer is that it is not impossible that some element of wisdom is present in these rites, even though we may not know it, since man cannot encompass God's wisdom in creation.

So much for the possibility and existence of the phenomenon of prophethood.[28]

As to the establishment of the prophethood of specific persons or person, the method is to know the ways of him whose prophethood we wish to ascertain, either by personal observation, or transmitted report, or hearsay. For example, if you know medicine and astronomy, you may recognize the physicians and astronomers by observing their ways and hearing their teachings. A reader of the books of Galen will not doubt his knowledge of medicine if the reader himself has studied some medicine. He who understands the meaning of prophethood, if he delves into what a claimant to prophethood has produced, and considers the reports about him and his ways, and what ritual practices and good deeds he prescribes, may on the basis of this, in addition to evidence that cannot be elaborated in detail, gain belief in the man's prophethood, dispensing with argumentation on any miraculous deeds performed by that man. The miracles by themselves may not be sufficient for belief in his prophethood as long as innumerable pieces of circumstantial evidence have not joined them, because there might be the suspicion of magic or illusion or God-willed error—for "God leads astray whom He will, and guides whom He will"[29]—or the other doubts about miracles. Rather, extraordinary events are but one of the proofs and evidences in the totality of consideration which leads to the assured knowledge about the prophethood of the particular prophet. Often certainty will result from the composite total, not from the particulars, as is the case of certainty about a

---

28. *Munqiḏ*, p. 43; *Guide*, Book II, chap. 40.

29. Koran, e.g., 14: 4; 16: 95.

transmitted report. This is the path to belief in the prophethood of prophets.

Prophethood has been claimed for innumerable persons, and it would be impossible for us to mention their circumstances and the proofs proffered. Every nation we know at present has one person or more for whom prophethood is claimed, except people of outlying regions and the like who resemble nonrational beings, yet whose economy and society
21 are integrated under some form of governance.

Thus the Magians claimed prophethood for Zarathustra, and held traditions about his numerous miracles. The Sabians claimed prophethood for Hermes, Agathodaemon, and others: it is reported that Hermes ascended into heaven, and many wise maxims were related in his name.[30] The Indians, the Turks, and others have personages for whom they claim prophethood and exalted rank. The Jews believe in the prophethood of Moses, upon whom be peace, and in the prophethood of prophets before him and of many prophets after him who upheld his religion. Similarly the Christians, who recognize all the foregoing and the prophethood of the Christ Jesus, son of Mary, peace upon him, claim that he is the son of God, that he is fully God and fully human. They abandoned the religion of Moses, and uphold the religion ascribed to Jesus. The Muslims

---

30. The Koran (2: 59 [62]; 5: 73 [69]; 22: 17) mentions the Sabians as a monotheistic group. Presumably it refers to the Judeo-Christian Mandaeans, "baptists" in Iraq. The name was used in the Islamic empire in the ninth to twelfth centuries by a group that was centered in Harran, used Aramaic, and persisted in a worship that represented a fusion of paganism, hellenistic gnosticism, and neopythagorean and neoplatonic speculation. While lower strata clung to pagan rites, the elite was rationalizing the old beliefs and cult, and, under increasing environmental pressure, framed them into a theoretical monotheism. The Sabians, through their scholarship and translations, influenced both Manichaeans and Muslims. Cf. J. B. Segal in E. Bacon, ed., *Vanished Civilizations* (New York, 1963); *id., Edessa and Harran* (London, 1963); articles by H. Lewy and F. Rosenthal in *A Locust's Leg: Studies in Honour of S. H. Taqizadeh* (London, 1962); F. Rosenthal, *Aḥmad b. aṭ-ṭayyib as-Saraḫsī* (New Haven, 1943), pp. 41–51; G. Widengren in *Handbuch der Orientalistik*, Abt. I, vol. 8, part 2 (Leiden and Cologne, 1961), pp. 98–100; B. Dodge in *American University of Beirut Festival Book* (1967).

believe in the prophethood of those recognized as prophets by the Jews and Christians, and believe, at the same time, in the prophethood of Muhammad, may God bless him and his kin, and they hold that his religion abrogates every previous religion. They oppose the Christians' tenet of Christ's divinity and that he is God's son, and they brand as infidel anybody maintaining that tenet.

As it is impossible to mention every claimant to prophethood and to mention the arguments for his prophethood, let us confine ourselves to the most important claimants widely known in our time and place, the arguments of the Jews, Christians, and Muslims about the prophethood of Moses, Jesus, and Muhammad, may they all be blessed. We shall examine thoroughly the questions concerning the arguments which have been brought up, devoting a chapter to each of these prophets.

# CHAPTER 2[1]

22 ## *Discussing briefly the proof of the Jews for the prophethood of Moses; the principles of the laws which he laid down for the Jews, as reported by them; questions and answers pertaining thereto.*

THE Jews say that divine power (*al-amr al-ilāhī*) attached itself first to Adam, father of mankind.[2] He was a prophet, and Abel was his successor. When Cain, envious of his brother's distinction, killed Abel, Seth, who was like Adam, was substituted for Abel; Seth was the essence of Adam, and the essence of Seth was then in Enosh. This divine power was thus passed down to Noah through individuals who formed an elite nucleus, perfect in physical constitution (*khalq*) and moral character (*akhlāq*), in longevity, and in knowledge and aptitude. Similarly, it continued from Noah to Abraham. There were among them, however, persons to whom the divine power did not attach itself, for example, Terach, Abraham's father. Abraham had the essence and was the disciple of his grandfather 'Eber, and therefore was called Hebrew.[3] 'Eber carried the essence of Shem and Shem of his father Noah. The essence of Abraham, among all his sons, was in Isaac, and Isaac's in Jacob, who is called Israel. Jacob's children were all of pure

1. A partial edition and translation of this chapter was published by Leo Hirschfeld: *Sa'd b. Manṣūr Ibn Kammūna und seine polemische Schrift* (Berlin, 1899). He stressed the dependence of the author upon Yehuda Hallewi's *Kitāb al-Khazarī*.

2. Cf. *Kh.*, Book I, par. 95, pp. 44 ff. On the theory of the divine power that attaches itself to mankind throughout generations, cf. the studies mentioned in the Introduction above, n. 7. Adam as prophet—cf. n. 9 below.

3. 'Eber = 'Ibrī, Hebrew.

essence, worthy of the divine power. God took heed to preserve them, to let them multiply and grow in Egypt, as a tree of good root will be cultivated until it produces as perfect a fruit as the original from which it was planted, that is, like Abraham, Isaac, and Jacob, and Joseph and his brethren. This fruit produced Moses, Aaron, Miriam, the chiefs of the tribes and the seventy elders who were fit for prophethood, Joshua the son of Nun, Caleb, Hur, and many others.

The Israelites were in bondage in Egypt.[4] The number of 23
their men was over 600,000, counting only those between the ages of 20 and 50—that is, not counting youth, boys, old men, and women—and they all were descended from the twelve sons of Jacob.

From their ancestors, they knew that a promise had been made that they would inherit Palestine. Palestine at that time was in the hands of seven extremely numerous, powerful, and prosperous nations, while the Israelites were suffering extreme humiliation and misery under Pharaoh who was slaying their children lest the Hebrews increase in number.

God then sent Moses and Aaron, though they were but two weak men. Moses was 80 years old when he was sent as prophet; Aaron was over 80. The two confronted Pharaoh, despite his power, with signs, miracles, and unusual acts. He could neither order any evil be done to them, nor protect himself from the ten plagues that befell the people of Egypt—their water, land, air, flora and fauna, their bodies, and their very lives. In an instant, at midnight, the most precious and beloved that the Egyptians had in their dwellings, namely all their first-born sons, died, and no dwelling other than those of the Children of Israel was without dead. The particulars of it are all mentioned in the Torah; therefore, I do not adduce them. Each of these plagues descended by divine will, with forewarning and threat, and likewise disappeared, so that it might be believed to have been ordained by a deity endowed with a will, who acts as he wills.

By divine command the Israelites came, that same night,

4. *Kh.*, Book I, par. 83, p. 34.

out of Pharaoh's house of bondage, and guided by a pillar of cloud and a pillar of fire that marched before them, set forth for the region of the Red Sea led by Moses and Aaron. Pharaoh and his host pursued them, but [the Israelites] did not have recourse to arms, nor were they of those that knew warfare. The sea split for them and they crossed it. Pharaoh and his host were drowned, and the sea washed them up dead before the Israelites so that the latter saw them with their own eyes.

Then the Israelites came to a barren wilderness.[5] Manna was sent to them day by day, except on the Sabbath, and they ate it for forty years. Then Moses died a natural death without illness or decrepitude when he had reached 120 solar years, as one who on a certain day at a certain hour retires to his couch to sleep. Nobody knows his tomb. His is of a rank essentially different from that of other humans.

24 Shortly after the Israelites left Egypt, God through Moses commanded them to prepare, by bodily and moral purification and by keeping aloof from their wives, for the divine speech that all of them would hear clearly, so that there should remain in their souls no doubt that God addresses human beings.[6] This came to pass after three days of their preparation; it was introduced by terrifying lightning, thunder, and earthquake, and a fire surrounded Mount Sinai. That fire over the mountain remained visible to the people for forty days; they saw Moses enter and emerge from it; they distinctly heard the delivery of ten commandments which are the very mainstay and source of the religions. God wrote these commandments on two tablets of precious stone and handed them over to Moses; thus the people saw them as divine scripture, even as they heard them in divine speech. By God's command, Moses made an ark for the commandments, and erected over it the Tent. This remained among the Israelites for about 900 years, until it disappeared as a result of their disobedience, when Nebuchadnezzar vanquished and exiled them.

The miracles performed by Moses were numerous and

---

5. *Ibid.*, par. 85, p. 38; par. 41, p. 20.
6. *Ibid.*, par. 87, pp. 38, 40.

great, such as changing his staff into a snake, turning his hand leprosy-white without damage, extracting water from the hard rock to quench the thirst of all the Israelites, bringing many quails to feed them, giving the people the shade of the cloud, shining the light over his countenance so that none could look at him and he had to cover his face when talking to people, and other miracles that are contained in the Holy Torah and related therein.

Every miracle of a post-Mosaic prophet in the religion of Moses, and on behalf of it, is like a Mosaic miracle, such as the one performed by the successor of Moses, Joshua the son of Nun. Upon his command the sun delayed setting until he had defeated his enemies, and the River Jordan dried up, and the flow of water was shut off until he had the ark and all the Israelites across the river. Such were the miracles performed by the prophet Elijah in reviving the son of the widow and in making the cruse of oil flow, in withholding the rains for three-and-a-half years, and in commanding the earth to remain barren. Later, Elijah offered a sacrifice and prayed to God, and He opened the gates of heaven and accepted the sacrifice, and rain fell down upon the earth, and the prophet seized his enemies, the idol-worshippers, and slew them upon Mount Carmel, after which God took him up to heaven in an act of grace. Such also were the acts of Elisha, who in his lifetime revived a corpse, and who again, after his death, revived another corpse as it touched his sepulchre. Such were the numerous miracles of the later prophets of the Mosaic religion, which are disclosed in their books and which would take too long to discuss here in detail.

One of the miracles of Moses is considered to be the promise he made in the Torah to the Israelites: if they were obedient, God would mark them by His solicitude and miracles, so that their sojourn in the Holy Land, which they had
been promised, would be perpetual. And the land's fertility 25
and barrenness, good and evil, would depend upon divine power, in accordance with the deeds of the Israelites, so that they would witness, through the presence of the holy spirit among them, the fertility of their land and the regularity of

rainfalls whose due seasons would not be retarded; despite inferior numbers, they would defeat their enemy. All of which would teach them that their affairs follow not a natural law but a divine will. Similarly, if they were disobedient, they would experience drought, famine, plague, ferocious beasts, and the like, while other people prospered, whereby they were to learn that their affairs were conducted by a force above the course of nature.[7]

That the course of their affairs was in accord with divine promise and warning is one of the great miracles of Moses. Most of his miracles were such as can hardly have resulted from illusion or a *consensus (tawāṭu')* to circulate such reports because they affected a large area of the earth and a great mass of people. Some of these miracles lasted as long as forty years. Only a few, such as turning the staff into a moving serpent, drawing out his hand all white, and the light on his face, were of short duration. If concerning the latter it might still be argued that they were produced by illusion, this does not apply to the former.

Moses brought to the Israelites the holy law but he did not abrogate the law that the nations had been commanded to observe since Adam and Noah.[8] He did not cancel it but reasserted the directive to observe it, and added to it that which distinguished the Israelites from other nations, and that which distinguished the tribe of Levi, especially Aaron and his progeny, by precepts and duties that did not apply to other Israelites.

For all the nations come under the obligation to observe what God commanded them through his prophets before Moses[9] as well as through Moses. The Israelites are bound by

---

7. *Ibid.*, par. 109, p. 58.

8. *Ibid.*, par. 83, p. 36; Book II, par. 97, p. 94. Cf. *JE*, VII, 648 ff. The Rabbis taught that some laws had been binding upon mankind at large, namely prohibition of: idolatry, adultery, murder, robbery, eating of a limb cut from a living animal, emasculation of animals, the pairing of animals of different species.

9. An Islamic notion that may well have had antecedents (e.g., in revering Abraham, David, and others as *prophets*).

what was prescribed unto the nations before Moses and by the added dispensations by which God distinguished them through his messenger Moses, as honour and solicitude for them. God favored Aaron and his sons by imposing additional duties upon them as a mark of distinction for them over the rest, which granted them special honor, status, and importance.

A gentile who undertook to observe the specific duties
imposed upon the Israelites, such as the Sabbath, and so on,
falls into the same category as the Israelites, so that should he
renounce those duties he would be liable to death. But God
did not allow anybody, be he Israelite or gentile, to join the
Aaronids, who were granted great distinction over other
people, and from among whom the high priest was specially 26
favored. He was the one to occupy the rank of Aaron in the
sanctuary, by virtue of additional duty and the distinction
over the rest of the Aaronids. It is thus clear that the addition
of duties corresponds to increased distinction, both in this
world and the hereafter.

All that God, through his faithful messenger Moses, commanded them was to believe in the oneness of God, to abandon idol-worship, to serve God alone, to exalt Him above any likeness, similarity, helper, or adviser, to worship Him exclusively, to love Him with all their hearts and souls and strength, to fear Him, ask His help, trust in Him, believe that He is omniscient and all-powerful, the Creator of everything; to believe that He brings death and life, disease and healing, and that there is no escape from His might; that He is the first and the last; that there is no God other than He. He commanded them to cultivate nobility of character, observe prayer and fast, give alms, practice justice and equity, respect contract and vow, honor parents and sages, obey and honor the rulers, and to wish unto others the good they wish unto themselves. He indicated to them the course to take in the conduct of home, public, and moral life. He forbade unto them vices and iniquities, murder, theft, adultery, and coveting other people's property. He also imposed upon them certain positive and negative injunctions whose purpose we are unable to fathom.

The permanently obligatory precepts and prohibitions of

the Torah amount to 613; in addition, there are commands and prohibitions that are not permanent and continuous. It would be too lengthy to go into detail; other books have dealt specially with the subject.

The Jews believe that the reward for obedience is eternal happiness in paradise and the world to come, while the punishment for disobedience is chastisement in gehenna; but there is no eternal punishment for the believer of this religion, even if he has been disobedient. Nothing thereof is clearly explicit in the Torah, for the reason that we shall mention; but the people's scholars, sages, and carriers of the religious tradition have transmitted the notion and have depicted paradise and hell, describing bliss and chastisement in great detail.

The Jews made it obligatory to mention in every prayer the belief in resurrection; stipulated that a prayer in which this was omitted was not valid; made it obligatory to mention
27 it daily even outside of prayer context and also at the site of a Jewish cemetery. They prescribed that a Jew sentenced to death should pray before his execution that it might be an expiation of his crime.[10]

Some of them believe that resurrection will occur twice: once at the time of their expected Messiah, which will affect the righteous of the community as a messianic miracle for the sake of those righteous persons; and once at the time of the resurrection of the dead on the general judgment day of all men, the righteous and the evil, to requite with eternal reward for obedience, and with retribution for refractoriness.

They also believe in the immortality of the soul after the destruction of the body, and the indestructibility of the soul, since this occurs in the books of the post-Mosaic prophets, and since such is the tradition of their rabbis and sages.

There have arisen among them those who assert that the world to come is merely the state after death; and that the eternal reward and retribution affect only the soul after the

---

10. Cf. *JE* s.v. *Resurrection.* Cemetery: TB *Berakhoṯ* 48*b*; execution: TB *Sanhedrin* 43*b*.

destruction of the body, and that neither reward nor retribution is corporeal but both are exclusively spiritual. Numerous texts transmitted on behalf of the sages and the authorities of the law speak metaphorically of reward and punishment, without reference to the return of the soul into the body. These texts, taken as a whole, do not lend themselves to any other interpretation by any thinking man.

By virtue of numerous Torah passages, and by reason of tradition, they believe that this religion will not be abrogated or superseded by another. They claim this is obvious from the law of Moses.

This, then, is an account by way of a summary of what the Jews believe concerning the prophethood of Moses and his message. Anyone who desires details should consult the Torah, the books of prophecy, and the writings of both the earlier and the more recent rabbis.

Seven objections have been raised against the tenets of Judaism.

**The first objection.**

The transmission [of the tradition] of the Jews is disrupted by the invasion of Nebuchadnezzar and other events; therefore, whatever you state concerning miracles and other matters is incorrect.

**Reply.**

This is sheer obstinacy, because he who learns their history to the extent the Jews themselves do cannot doubt that the Hebrew language, which none but they speak, is the same as that spoken at the beginning of their history, nor will he doubt the reality of Moses and Aaron, of David and Solomon,
and of their other famous kings. He will conclude that their 28
well-known prophets and the generations of sages responsible for their theology and jurisprudence did exist; and he will not doubt the period of the existence of the Temple from the time it was built by Solomon until it was destroyed, and the period of the existence of the Temple that was built after that, the kingdom of the Hasmonaeans, the destruction of the Second Temple by Titus, the particulars of the Jews' history, learning,

jurisprudence, and other matters that are transmitted only by the Jews.

Even if the transmission had been disrupted, we should not reach any such negative conclusion.

Even the massacres perpetrated among them by Nebuchadnezzar and others, are no proof of the breakdown of the transmission of Jewish tradition. Did not the Persians defeat the Byzantines, kill their men, and maltreat their progeny? Likewise, the Greeks came to Persia in the days of Alexander, slew its king Darius, razed its fortresses, and destroyed its scriptures. The Arabs were invaded by the Ethiopians, who slew them and occupied their land until the king of Persia sent a force to rout the Ethiopians. What is more, not all the Jews were in Jerusalem when Nebuchadnezzar conquered it, nor did he slay every person in that city.

For in the Book of Jeremiah it states that the mass of the Israelites left safely.[11] They were to be found subsequently in many lands, and prophecy continued among them for some 110 years.

Even their enemies who attack their religion testify in a way that precludes the notion of a breakdown in their transmission.

Thus the author of the book *Ifḥām al-Yahūd* stated in his work as follows:[12]

> The Jews in ancient times used to call their legists "sages." These legists had academies in Babylonia, Syria, Ctesiphon, and Palestine, the like of which no other people had. They had thousands of legists at a time, under the rule of the Nabat (the Babylonians) Persians, Greeks, and Romans.

If such was their state after the assault of Nebuchadnezzar, how then could Nebuchadnezzar have slain them to the extent that a sufficient number for transmission of tradition was not left among them? Later on, following the assault of Nebuchadnezzar, they had a Great Assembly, whose reality cannot be

---

11. Jer. 52: 12–15, 28–30.
12. Samau'al, pp. 71 f./64.

doubted by anyone who learns the detailed lives of its members as known to the Jews. The construction of the Second
Temple occurred 70 years after the assault mentioned, and at
that time the Jews were a multitudinous people. He who is
unbiased and not deliberately obdurate will definitely recognize that the transmission of their tradition had not broken
down as a whole, but only concerning certain situations and
events because of the long lapse of time. Also because they did
not consider these things important, interest in them was 29
limited and these points became the subject of transmission
by but few individuals or were altogether forgotten; this is
not peculiar to the Jews alone among the nations.[13]

**The second objection.**[14]

Even if we admit the original veracity of their transmission, we still do not admit the transmission of the Torah because memorizing it was not a duty nor a custom among them, except that each of the Aaronids would memorize one chapter. When Ezra saw that the people's Temple was burnt, their statehood ended, their mass dispersed, and their scripture destroyed, he collected, from what he remembered and from chapters remembered by the priests, the stuff from which he concocted this Torah that is preserved by the Jews. He may have added to or subtracted from it, in accordance with his purpose, so that in truth it is a book by Ezra, not a divine book.

This argument is strengthened by the fact that when a state perishes, its true records are wiped out, and its monuments are obliterated by successive invasions, warfare, and destruction of the land.[15] And this nation of the Jews was overwhelmed by the Babylonian Chaldaeans, Persians, Greeks, Christians, and Muslims, each nation seeking to hurt it in the extreme. Even more injurious to the Jews than all these kingdoms was what they suffered at the hands of their own rebellious kings, who worshiped idols, and built huge sanctuaries and temples for them. The kings and the majority of the

---

13. End of section published by Hirschfeld (see n. 1, above).

14. Cf. Samau'al, pp. 50 f./54 f.

15. *Ibid.*, pp. 54 f./56 f.

Israelites applied themselves to the cult of the idols, and for long periods over successive centuries abandoned the stipulations and faith of the Torah. If such was the succession of calamities that their religion sustained from their own kings and at their own hands, what, then, is one to think of the various calamities that later followed one after another under the domination of the other nations? It is in the records of one of their kings that a copy of the Torah found in the Temple was brought to him; he read it, and ordered that Passover be observed. In the story of Ezra it states that when he read the Torah in the assembly of the community, and they found in the text the stipulation concerning the Feast of the Tabernacles, and the prohibition of marriage with the daughters of Ammon and Moab, they accordingly built tabernacles and divorced the women who were from Ammon and Moab. This is proof that they had previously lost the Torah.[16]

**Reply.**

As to the opponents' view that memorizing the Torah was neither an obligation nor a custom among the Jews, the Torah preserved by the Jews at present speaks to the contrary, as do also their law books.

The opponents say that this Torah is not the original Torah but one distorted and changed, yet they prove its distortion by quoting from that same distorted text. This is nonsense and claim without proof. Even if memorizing the Torah should be neither obligatory nor prescribed, this does not impair transmission, because among the Jews it is a great book from which they derive their religion; their legal cases make it necessary to memorize the book, be meticulous about it, and argue by quoting it; and above all they delight in reading it, and exalt it in their worship.

We find that if books written by people are well thought of and prove useful, they will enjoy good transmission for

---

16. II Kings 23: 21–23; Ezra 9: 1–5, 10–14; 10: 10 ff.; Neh. 13: 13–29. Tabernacles: Ezra 3: 4–6; Neh. 8: 13–18. (Ezra and Neh. counted as one book in the Hebrew text.)

hundreds of years. This is even more true in the case of a book believed to be the word of God.

The Jews indeed kept the Torah and the books of their prophets with a meticulousness we do not find in any other people toward any other book. They counted its verses, its words, and its letters—every letter of the text. They did this with each of its books, with each section of each book; they even stated about every word, or about many of the words, whether it does or does not occur again—and if it does, how many times, in which passage, whether in the middle, or beginning, or end of the verse—and developed other such admirable precision devices. Special books, well-known among the Jews, were written on the subject. Often they wrote these notes on the margins of their bible volumes. This is well-known among them.

Further, the Jews are divided into a number of sects which differ from one another in secondary matters but not about the Torah or the prophetic books. And although the sects differ in the interpretation of some passages, they do not differ in the wording and sequence of the text.

All this disposes of the suspicion that the text has been
distorted and tampered with. But if it be said that the Torah 31
in the possession of the Christians differs from that of the Jews, and that the Samaritan text differs from the other two versions, all of which might strengthen the case of those who claim that the text has been tampered with and distorted, we should say:

The Christians do not have the Torah in the original language of revelation, that is, in Hebrew, but in a Syriac translation which is available among them in two versions; one is like that of the Jews except for a few words in the interpretation of which there is some difference, and which the translator rendered in the other language according to his own notion of their meaning; and the other version, called the Septuagint, differs also in a few words, and to no considerable extent on the computation of ages in the early chapters of the Torah. That is only because the Christians do not worship by reading the Torah and other prophetic writings to the extent that the Jews do, or even nearly so; and therefore, with some of the Christians, negligence occurred in copying or translating it into a foreign tongue, as happens with many works when copyists neglect to check, or for some other reason.

The same is true of the Samaritan version. It differs slightly from the two other versions because at first the Samaritans did not use it in worship, and later, after making an inexact and ill-edited translation, they then decided to use it in worship. That is how it has remained among them.

The three versions of the Torah show only a few words of variant meaning, and the variation is much slighter than that found in the seven readings of the Koran, or in the Koran versions of Ibn Mas'ūd and Ubayy, and so on.

Yet the Jewish sects do not differ about even a single word in the Torah, or in the prophetic books in their possession, or about the miracles of Moses, or the wording of the Law. Nor is there any difference about it among the three communities, that is, Jews, Samaritans, or Christians.

The notion of an agreement among the Jews of various lands to alter the text is obviously not acceptable to any sound mind. Even if it were possible, those of other nations who embraced Christianity would not agree with them, such as the Byzantines, Franks, Aramaic-speaking people, Armenians, Greeks, Copts, Indians, Ethiopians, Arabs, Nubians, Daylamis, Berbers, Khazars, Slavs, and Chinese.[17] The more so because both Jews and Christians are split into various and conflicting groups.

Should they say that the Torah had been tampered
32 with prior to the rise of Christianity and its wide diffusion, it might be said in reply: if that were so, then Christ and the Apostles would have made this known, and would have prohibited reading the Torah, referring to it, and quoting from it, and from the other prophetic books as well. But it is known that the opposite is true.

17. "Berbers": the text has, perhaps, Sadīr; the Chinese are followed by Swds. These are unclear points. Presumably this is a quotation from an earlier text. (There were no Khazars in Ibn Kammūna's time.)

Further, prophethood continued among the people during the second commonwealth for forty years, and this Torah was in use among them, down to the appearance of Jesus, for over 300 years. Throughout that period, too, the Jews were of various factions and numerous sects.

Ezra, to whom the opponents ascribe the reintroduction of the Torah after its alleged disappearance, is famous for reverence, great righteousness, and piety. It is he whom the Muslims called 'Uzayr; they and some of the Jews claim he was a prophet, but even those who question his prophethood do not question his great righteousness and piety. Therefore it cannot be imagined that he would have permitted himself to tamper with and distort the divine scripture.[18]

The opponents refer to the kings of the Jews as idol-worshipers who built sanctuaries for their idols. This occurred not out of unbelief in God, or the Torah, or Moses, but, rather, it has been said, by reason of the kings' pursuit of immediate advantages through special procedures commended by astrologers and magicians. Yet they observed the stipulations and fundamentals of their faith. The better kings destroyed those sanctuaries so that only the God-chosen temple might be honored. Although the idol-worship amounted to a major sin against the faith, the sin was disregarded by the rebellious kings of that time because it was common practice among all the peoples to worship images and claim that these were invested with divine power. This is considered so abominable at present only because it has disappeared among most peoples in our time and our lands.[19]

As to the story of the scroll found in the Temple and the resulting royal decree to celebrate Passover, this happened not because the Torah had not been available until that scroll was found, nor because its stipulations had been forgotten; rather, they say, that the scroll was unrolled on a verse from which the king might derive an omen, and whenever they unrolled it for another verse, they found that it still pointed to that par-

---

18. 'Uzayr: cf. *SEI*; Koran 9: 30.

19. *Kh.*, Book I, par. 97, pp. 46, l. 24, 50, ll. 14 f., 22. Cf. p. 147.

ticular one, so that they understood it was a sign and warning from God. That is what is said. But perhaps there is another explanation thereof.[20]

As to those who had bestirred themselves to divorce their wives of Ammonite and Moabite descent as well as to erect the tabernacles for the festival [only] after Ezra had read the Torah to them, they were but a fraction of the Jews, those who had mixed with other peoples, not the nation as a whole.

There were at the time prophets, saints, sages, many distinguished Aaronids and Levites, and members of the Great Assembly who transmitted the law and the faith, and are [still]
33 authoritative for the Jews' legal stipulations and legal opinions. How can it then be imagined that all these were ignorant of the Torah? This is utterly improbable, from the outset. It would be more to the point if the opponent confined himself to refuting the transmission of the Torah prior to the erection of the Second Temple.

**The third objection.**

In the Torah text current among the Jews we find many passages indicative of anthropomorphism and anthropopathy, describing God in unworthy terms, and other signs of blasphemy which sound minds will reject and deny as incredible. It is then impossible that this be divinely revealed matter. Such are the reports that Moses and the elders of his people ascended into the mountain where they beheld God; or that God created man in His own image; or that Noah, upon leaving the ark, built an altar for God, and offered sacrifices upon it, whereupon God scented the savor; or that the two tablets were written with God's finger. They ascribe to God regret, anger, love, and speaking with voice and word, things unworthy of Him.[21]

---

20. II Kings 22: 8–13; 23: 21–23. The author's view goes back to the Talmud (*Yoma* 52b) where it is related that King Josiah (in 621 B. C.) was struck by the passage in Deut. 28:36: "The Lord will bring thee and thy King . . . unto a nation that thou hast not known . . ." The commentary of Kimhi mentions this explanation.

21. Samau'al, pp. 44–48.

**Reply.**

The prohibition of anthropomorphism and anthropopathy is mentioned in a number of passages of the Torah. The second of the Ten Commandments inscribed on the tablets is the prohibition against having any deity but God, and against representing, likening, and picturing Him.

As to the elders beholding God,[22] it has been said that, though it occurred in a waking state, it was like beholding in a dream as opposed to the external sense. The trenchant proof thereof is that when God, in another passage of the Torah forbade anthropomorphism and warned them against holding such beliefs, He reminded them that they had not seen any image on *that* occasion. He simply denied true vision with the seeing eye. Thus it is clear that the vision mentioned in this passage is not that of normal sight. It is possible because God in His subtlety established a relationship between internal perception and the nonmaterial, and granted to whomever He honored among His creatures an internal eye to see things, and an intellect to perceive the meaning and essence of these things. He who is granted such vision has true insight. Perhaps this
internal eye is the imagining power that serves the rational 34
power: it sees an overwhelming image pointing to verities beyond doubt. Just as you cannot grasp the sense of the words of prayer by mere cogitation, without recitation; just as you cannot grasp the number 100, for example, without word, especially if you want to combine it with various other numbers; so also, were it not for that sense that maintains rational order through images and similes, this order could not be maintained. Such, possibly, was the state that came over Moses and the elders of the Israelites, from the impact of the glory of God, when they beheld the glory and radiance of that image created for them and the awesome phenomena that accompanied the vision. We are like the blear-eyed who, unable to behold the light, follow the seeing who are able to behold it. The vision of images as experienced in dream or in the waking

22. Exod. 24: 10 vs. Deut. 4: 15. Cf. *Kh.*, Book IV, par. 3, p. 238, ll. 15 f.

state, even if the images are not real, facilitates imagination thereof and eliminates the suspicion of its improbability, even though the relation between the two kinds of perception (the sensory and the inner) is remote. Just as word and voice are descriptive of God's speech—that which is neither word nor voice, but is called God's speech—so this image that God created for the prophets and saints to see, and which indicates the glory and majesty of God, is called, figuratively, God; and there is no danger therein as long as there is no belief in corporeality, anthropomorphism, or incarnation, as has been pointed out earlier, in the discussion of the mysteries of the miracles of the prophets and the images they behold.[23]

Thus the problem of God creating man in His image is solved. Though the expression "the image" may be employed, it is not shape and design that are meant, and presumably such is not its intent here. Other interpretations have been given of beholding God and of the creation of Adam in God's image, but there is no need to go into these.

Concerning the scenting of the savor of the sacrifices,[24] it is an expression for the acceptance of the sacrifices, just as the sentence, "God heard his prayer" means "He accepted it." "The finger of God" is a metaphor for His power, just as "the hand" is used metaphorically for this same meaning in both Hebrew and Arabic. This is proved conclusively in the Torah story about the Egyptians; when they were stricken by the plagues, they said: This is the finger of God.[25] Of course they meant the might of God. He who does what a repentant among us will do will be called "repentant" metaphorically. Yet the Torah and the prophetic books state that repentance cannot be imputed to God. It is necessary then to interpret the repentance ascribed to Him. Thus when God destroyed the creatures by flood, He announced beforehand that He would destroy them, and this was expressed by the statement that He repented having created them, after the fashion of one who

---

23. *Kh.*, Book I, par. 5, 7, p. 246, ll. 15–20; p. 248, l. 15.

24. Gen. 8: 21.

25. Exod. 31: 18; Exod. 8: 19.

repents a deed and seeks to rectify the situation by discontinuing his deed, and by showing anger about it.[26]

The angry person will take revenge upon him who an- 35
gered him. That is why retribution by God is called anger. As the loving among us will show much concern and pity for those they love, God's mercy and His strong concern is called "love"; but not because He experiences the emotions of the angry person or the loving one. God is sublimely above that.

Divine speech in voice and word has been discussed above. All such passages in the Torah and the other books of the Jewish prophets, and in the books of the rabbis and sages, should be interpreted in a similar vein. Later Jewish authors wrote books elucidating the point, and others like it, in greater detail.[27]

**The fourth objection.**

The Torah which is available at present contains stories that sound minds will dismiss—nay, consider impossible, such as the story of Adam and the reason for his leaving Paradise, and the stories of Lot and of Judah. Also it contains stories whose telling is pointless, such as the story of the branching out of tribes from Noah, with their names and places, and also of the children of Seir, and the enumeration of the kings who ruled in Edom, the number of stations in the march of the Israelites to Palestine, and so on. There also occur in it legal stipulations that seem to make no positive sense. The mind refuses to accept that such should issue from the Most Wise or that they should be announced by a prophet who was addressed by God Himself.

This view is strengthened by the story at the end of the Torah concerning the death of Moses, how he was buried, and how his sepulchre remained unknown. Now, reason reveals it as unlikely that this should have been announced to Moses in a divine revelation, in the past tense, while he was yet alive.

**Reply.**

We do not agree that the stories of Adam, Lot, and Judah are rationally unlikely, especially in that [distant] time. For

---

26. Gen. 6: 6.

27. Presumably an allusion to *Kh.* and *Guide.*

conventions change with time, and what is considered unlikely to have happened in one period, may be considered feasible in another.[28]

With respect to the objection that some biblical stories are not worth mentioning, it is not conceded that they were devoid of sense at the time of revelation, or for a past or a future time.

As for the genealogies and tribes, perhaps they were mentioned in order that it should not seem unlikely that there has
36 been such a branching out of mankind throughout the world in the short period between Noah and Moses, and to dispel doubt should it arise. This doubt was accordingly disposed of by the genealogies and their ramifications by naming the famous men among them, their ages and abodes.[29]

As to the tribes of the children of Seir, perhaps these were enumerated because of the commandment to exterminate the progeny of Amalek, the son of Eliphaz. Esau, the brother of Jacob, married into the progeny of Seir, had children by them, reigned over them, and his descendants mingled with theirs. The whole land of Seir and those tribes became known as related to the major tribe, the Children of Esau, and particularly to the descendants of Amalek. Therefore Scripture identified their tribes, lest in the battle against Amalek some other tribe should suffer. There may be other points about all this, points that escape us at present, but if we knew them and the circumstances of the time, we would understand fully why they are mentioned. No doubt the deeds and fates of those kings were well-known. Perhaps they were included so that their histories might serve as warnings.[30]

As to the stations of the Israelites on their way to the promised land, perhaps their list is included in order to establish the miracle of their forty-year sojourn in the wilderness, the daily finding of the manna in that wilderness so far from cultivation, devoid of water and tilled soil, and infested

---

28. Gen. 3, 19, 38.
29. Cf. *Guide*, Book III, chap. 50.
30. Gen. 36.

with poisonous snakes and insects. During that period the Israelites did not eat bread. These are clear and evident miracles. God knew that, in the future, these miracles would fare as did other historical reports; that it might be thought that the Israelites had sojourned in a desert close enough to cultivation that man could dwell there, such as the steppes of the Arabs and of the Turks; or that it could have been cultivated; or that the manna, which was the greatest miracle, was readily available there; or that there were water wells in the wilderness. All such suspicions were eliminated by the mention of those stations and abodes, so that men in the future could view them and understand the great miracle of the people's sojourn in those places for forty years.

For a similar reason, Joshua the son of Nun prohibited for all time the rebuilding of Jericho in order to preserve the miracle, so that all might see that wall sunk in the ground and understand clearly that such a structure can be destroyed only by a miracle and not by acts of nature.[31]

The irregular spacing of the stations, the return to some 37
of them, the stays of varying lengths—18 years at one station, one day or one night at another, in accordance with the rise of the pillar of cloud—all this was mentioned to indicate that it had occurred with divine help, and was not aimless wandering on the road as some people think today. For, it is known that that area can be crossed in a march of 11 days. How then could that great mass of people wander there for forty years?[32]

Not a single story is mentioned in the Torah that does not have evident religious significance. Either it is helpful in correcting an idea or practice important for the integration of society or in some other respect.

As to the irrational stipulations, it does not necessarily follow because we do not understand their meaning that they are essentially without meaning, for as stated above, we cannot fathom all the hidden wisdom of God. Yet it is not im-

---

31. *Guide, loc. cit.*; Josh. 6: 26.

32. *Guide, loc. cit.*, p. 122*b*. Cf. Nu. 9:21. The figure *18 years* is a rabbinic computation (*Seder Olam Rabba* VIII).

probable that the people of those times did know the sense [of the stipulations].

The point is that this religion arose while the Ṣabian faith prevailed.[33] Now, whoever studies the Ṣabian systems, views, acts, and ritual will clearly understand the motivation behind many of the Torah precepts whose sense is not obvious. You can learn those systems and views from the books compiled by the Ṣabians, such as the book on Nabatean agriculture edited by Ibn Waḥshīya, a book replete with the ravings of idol-worshipers and acts of magic and sorcery of *jinns* and *ghuls* inhabiting the wilderness;[34] or the book *al-Ustumakhus* attributed to Aristotle; or the books on magic, such as *Tumtum, Sarb, The Degrees of the Sphere and the Constellations rising by degree*; or a book on magic ascribed to Aristotle; or a book attributed to Hermes; or the book of Isḥāq the Ṣābian in his defense of the Ṣabian faith, and his larger work on their laws and the details of their religion, festivals, sacrifices, prayers, and so on. Many such books have been translated into Arabic, there are many times more that have not.[35]

A distinguished and venerable author explained the reason behind most of the Torah precepts, in general and in particular, from what he gleaned from these books. I will mention here the gist of his general discussion, without going into detail about each and every precept. Although his approach is very applicable and suitable, I still do not conclude
38 and decide that these precepts are motivated accordingly; nay, possibly God's wisdom therein was even greater and more inscrutable than suggested by this scholar, which is more likely and plausible.

He said, in substance, that just as God showed subtle graciousness in the creation of living beings, in the gradation of the motions of the limbs and in the mutual proximity

33. Cf. *Ibid.*, chap. 29.

34. A tenth-century work that was supposed to be a translation of ancient Chaldean wisdom. The works mentioned in this passage issued apparently from the Harranian center of the Ṣabians. Cf. chap. 1, n. 30, above.

35. This is quoted from *Guide, loc. cit.*, p. 66; the next passage alludes to Maimonides.

of the limbs, so He showed it in the successive stages of the individual as a whole. Thus, He made the front part of the brain soft, its rear more solid. The spinal marrow is even more solid, and becomes more and more solid the farther it extends. The nerves are the organ of sensation and motion; thus the nerves required only for apprehension by the senses or for a slight motion, such as the motion of the eyelid or the jaw, issue from the brain, while those required for moving the limbs issue from the spinal marrow. As it is impossible for a nerve, because of its softness—even a nerve issuing from the spinal marrow—to set a joint in motion, God subtly allowed the nerve to be solidified by the hardened muscle, to be combined with fragments of ligaments, and to become a tendon attached to the bone, clinging to it, with the ability to set the limb in motion, all owing to this gradation. God showed His subtle graciousness toward a suckling living being. As it is extremely tender when born, no dry food is suitable for it; He therefore provided that the mother's breasts yield milk so that the young might be fed liquid food suitable for the formation of its limbs until gradually the limbs become firm and solid.[36]

God proceeded similarly, in revealing the sacred law, for it was revealed at a time when the well-known traditional pattern was to offer sacrifices of various living beings to images in sanctuaries, and to prostrate oneself and burn incense before these images. Wisdom did not dictate that the faith should begin by rejecting and abandoning all such habits. Given man's predilection for what is customary and his aversion to what contradicts it, which are natural human tendencies, such a religious law might even be rejected. Thus, if a prophet were now to call us to abandon prayers and fasts, to refrain from calling upon God in time of distress, and to worship Him solely in pure meditation, we would detest it and reject it. 39
Divine wisdom and subtlety dictated that some old rites of worship and the strange acts connected with them be per-

36. *Ibid.*, Book III, chap. 32. Divine graciousness (*talaṭṭuf*), includes a measure of wile and subtle foresight toward producing a certain effect.

mitted to continue—acts for which beneficial properties are claimed, as for those performed by magic-workers; but God diverted the worship of objects, planets, or spiritual principles to worship in His name, and commanded that it be performed for Him. He therefore commanded that a sanctuary be erected for Him and that the altar, sacrifice, and incense be dedicated to Him. He also forbade the performance of such acts with respect to any other deity. He singled out the Aaronid priests and the Levites to serve that sanctuary, and set dues to ensure a maintenance for their work in the sanctuary and the sacrificial rite. Thus the true creed was firmly established, namely the existence of God and His oneness, without men rebelling or feeling repugnance at the abolition of the familiar modes of worship. As worship by sacrifice and the like pertains to the secondary intent [of religion] whereas prayer, supplication and the like are closer to the primary intent and necessary thereto, God emphatically separated the two kinds of worship from each other: sacrifices, even though offered to God, were no longer to be offered as they once were, that is, at any time or place, nor is a sanctuary to be erected just anywhere, or the offering made by anybody; God set for worship one sanctuary, and forbade sacrifices at any other, and the offerer must be only of the progeny of Aaron. This was all done to restrict this [older] form of worship. But prayer and supplication and the like could be offered anywhere, by anybody. Just as the true faith preserved the style of worship which people had used to make offerings to others than God, so the true faith also aimed at opposing most of the former cult's particulars in order that alienation from that cult might take place within the framework of the necessary limited approval, in accordance with human welfare and the subtle divine plan. This is so precisely because the foundation of this true faith, the pivot upon which it revolves, is the eradication of the old notions from people's minds and the elimination of those false rites.[37] Thus the motivation of much of what seems irrational in Mosaic legislation

37. *Ibid.*, chap. 29, p. 66*b*, bottom.

becomes clear only to him who knows the faith, cult, and specific rites of the Sabians and of the other idol-worshipers.

Furthermore, one of the goals of the perfect law is to induce man to repudiate his desires, scorn them, restrict them to a minimum. Divine subtlety is manifest in the stipulations of precepts that nullify this concern for the senses as a goal, deflect thought entirely from them, and preclude anything that leads to mere pleasure and lust—alimentary and sexual.[38]

It is also an intent of the law to foster gentleness and 40
patience: man should be not violent, cruel, and coarse but responsive, humble, repentant, forbearing, compassionate, and affectionate. Much of the law, if you examine it, will be found to lead to this goal. The outer cleansing of filth and impurity, after the inner cleansing of moral vice and purificaton by positive morals, is also the aim of religion. One cannot fail to see the many benefits stemming from the precepts that lead in this direction. Such is the overall motivation. The detailed motivation would be too long. Whenever the benefits of a precept are disclosed, they are substantial. This refutes the assertion of those who reject the divine origin of such precepts.[39]

As to the denial that the account of his death and burial was revealed to Moses, it has been said that Joshua the son of Nun was commanded by God to write this account and to include it at the end of the Torah.[40] Still, the revelation of the account to Moses is neither unfeasible nor incredible. Often the past tense is used metaphorically—to describe the future as if it has already taken place—to lend certainty to a foreseeable event.

**The fifth objection.**

In this Torah we do not find a clear statement about reward and punishment in the hereafter, even though this most important matter needs mention because it is a cardinal principle in founding a religion. If the Torah [currently] in the possession of the Jews were a divine revelation, it would not

---

38. *Ibid.*, chap. 33, beginning.

39. *Ibid.*, p. 73*b*.

40. TB *Baba Baṯra* 15*a*, concerning Deut. 34: 5.

omit a statement on this subject nor dwell instead on worldly reward and punishment, as it so often does. The world is transitory, its pleasure and wretchedness not to be reckoned with. Even if we should reckon with it, experience dictates the conclusion that pleasure in the world is not limited to the good, nor is wretchedness therein confined to the sinners. Rather, many a good, law-abiding man is wretched, and many an iniquitous and godless man is fortunate. God is too far above mankind to be concerned with promises of bliss and warnings of chastisement in this world, nor would He announce events that fail to occur or of which the opposite occurs.

**Reply.**

If Moses received a revelation on the subject [of reward and punishment in the hereafter], spoke about it to the Israelites, and from them the matter spread further, then it is of no great import that the Torah omits a clear statement on it.

If it is asked why he did not write about it in the Torah, the reply could be: In divine matters there can be no opposing or questioning, as they may contain wisdom of which we have no knowledge.

41 Furthermore, the prophets are physicians of the soul by God's guidance.[41] Just as the physician of the body treats only the disease present in the body, so the physician of the soul, that is, the prophet, treats the disease of man's soul in accordance with what he finds in his time. People in the time of Moses did not deny reward and punishment in the hereafter; their disease was the worship of idols and planets, and the like—in

---

41. Prophets as physicians of the soul. This wide-spread idea has hellenistic antecedents going back to the idea of the philosopher-king. It is strong in the Epistles of the Sincere Brethren and in Ghazali. Later a genre of prophetic medicine (*al-ṭibb al-nabawī*) combines notions of psychology-psychiatry, admonitions and spiritual discipline for individual and communal training, with a theological-anthropological notion on the divine scheme for human intellectual and social advancement, and the role of the prophet within this scheme. For beginning of passage, cf. *Munqiḏ*, p. 46; continuation adapts *Guide*, Book III, chap. 30.

short, the worship of forces other than God, and the belief that by worshiping these forces and offering sacrifices to them the earth would become cultivated, the land fertile, and the trees fruitful. The learned, pious, and religious, admonished the people and taught them that agriculture, which is the basis of human existence, "will succeed and bring bliss if you worship the sun and the planets, but if you enrage them by your disobedience, the land will be desolate and waste." Their books, mentioned above, stated that the wilderness and desert areas angered Jupiter, and that that is why they became waterless, treeless, the habitation of demons. The books greatly extolled the plowman, the tiller of the soil, for cultivating the soil in accordance with the will and pleasure of the planets. The *Book of Nabatean Agriculture*[42] contains a Sabian discourse on the vineyard to the effect that all the ancient thinkers as well as the prophets have commanded and enjoined that during festivals the people should play musical instruments before the idols; for the gods are pleased by it, and would reward handsomely those who do so. The Sabians were profuse in assurance [of reward] and warning [of punishment] therefor; that is, they promised long life, fertility of the fields, abundant crops, and elimination of calamities and blights. When these beliefs spread and were believed to be true, and God, in His mercy, wished to erase this error from the minds and to lift this burden from men's bodies by abolishing those exacting and useless actions, He announced through His prophet Moses that if those planets and idols continued to be worshiped, rain would cease, the earth would be waste and barren, the trees' fruit would be lost, calamities and blights would affect bodies, and the life-span would be shortened; whereas the worship of God would make the rains plentiful, the earth fertile, conditions favorable, the body healthy, and the life-span long. He repeated these assurances and threats in several passages in the Torah, so that the wrong notion might vanish, be entirely erased from the souls, which could then recover from the disease and corruption caused by this creed.

---

42. Cf. n. 34, above.

If their disease had been the denial of the immortality of the soul beyond death, denial of reward and punishment in the hereafter, He would have repeatedly mentioned it in the Torah for emphasis and affirmation. But as that was not the case, He was satisfied with the diffusion of this view among the people through mere allusion to the matter.

42 Thus the Jews believed in resurrection, acknowledged immortality of the soul after the death of the body, and transmitted the tradition thereof from one generation to another. They pray over their dead, yield to repentance when they believe the end is near, and teach one who is to be executed in punishment or retaliation to beg, before his execution, that God make his death an expiation for his sin, so that he might be free from chastisement in the hereafter. They make the mention of belief in resurrection obligatory in prayer and out and when passing a Jewish cemetery, as mentioned above in the account of their creed. Their rabbis and sages however, have made mention of many particulars concerning paradise and hell, systematizing them repeatedly.

If it is asked: why is it that the fulfillment of the assurance to the obedient and of the warning to the disobedient is not continuous in this world so that it may serve as evidence in the refutation of the worshipers of idols and planets, it may be said: it was fulfilled as long as the Divine Presence was among the people so that they might know that they lived under a law willed by God, who was concerned about them, and, as was stated earlier, not under a natural law as did others. In this world the assurance and warning are not unconditional. They are addressed to the community of the Hebrews as a whole, as an entity, and in that particular country which they were promised when the Divine Presence dwelled among them, there and not elsewhere, nor to any person on an individual basis. The assurance [of reward] to individuals according to their obedience and the warning [of punishment] according to their disobedience refer exclusively to the hereafter, to judgement after death. In this world, however, assurance and warning do not operate consistently. Sometimes divine concern for a righteous and good person can be detected

in his specific advantageous position in the world; and as for the suffering caused by the iniquitous to themselves and to others, the intelligent observer will undoubtedly recognize much of it as punishment meted out to them for their iniquity. But it is not always thus, for we find in this world a fortunate man who is refractory and an unfortunate man who is obedient to God, as the Jews' sages and traditionists have admitted. The fulfillment of the assurance to the community, in the case of its obedience, has been experienced, as well as that of the warning, in the case of its disobedience and deviation into worship of idols and celestial bodies in the quest for worldly benefits. This becomes clear on looking into the history of the kings and prophets of the Jews, and into the history of their elders in the Holy Land that they inherited, at the time when the Divine Presence was dwelling among them. A Jewish author likened the people of Israel to a living people, and other peoples to the dead.[43] If the non-Jews wished to become like the Jews they could but achieve an external resemblance; thus they erected houses for God but no trace of His presence
appeared in them; they practiced asceticism and penitence so 43
that inspiration might be granted to them, but it was not granted; they were dissolute, disobedient, wicked, yet no divine punishment came upon them, such as a sure sign that it was in retribution for this disobedience that their heart was affected—I mean, their temple toward which they turned in their prayers. Their status did not change; whether they were numerous or few, strong or weak, in discord or accord, their status did not veer from the course of nature and accident. But in the Jewish community, once its heart, the Temple, was affected, the whole community was crushed; if the Temple be restored, they, too, will be restored, be they many or few, whatever be their status. Their ruler and supporter in their dispersion and exile is the living God. For dispersion such as the one to which the Jews were exposed, especially in view of its long duration, is inconceivable in any other nation without

43. This refers to Yehuda Hallewi. The whole paragraph adapts *Kh.*, Book II, par. 32–33, p. 100.

a loss of identity. Many a nation that arose after them has perished without leaving a trace.

Such is the substance of the discussion of this subject.

**The sixth objection.**

Numerous miracles have been reported, on the strength of a continuous tradition, concerning Zoroaster and many others who claimed prophethood in the other nations. Yet the Jews deny their prophethood, especially the prophethood of idol-worshipers. If that is the case, the Jews must be told:

The tradition of these claimants is either true or not true. If it is not, what makes you sure that your tradition about the miracles of Moses and the affairs of your religion is? For your transmission is neither stronger than theirs, nor sounder. If their tradition is sound, miracle is no proof of being in the right; then the prophethood of Moses and of your other prophets is no proof in your favor.[44]

**Reply.**

Unless their transmission be known, reports of the extraordinary phenomena wrought by a challenger [= claimant to prophethood] represent no proof. Part of what is said to have been wrought by those who urge people to worship fire, planets, and idols falls into this category. But not everything in vogue through tradition in a mighty nation has been reliably transmitted. Vogue is not the same as transmission, and the difference between the two is clearly stated in books on logic. If a certain report is *reputed* to be known by transmission, that is not to say that it actually *is* known by transmission. Lack of such differentiation is a pitfall that may give rise to serious errors in terms of reference. Nor can anything known
44 to have enjoyed continuous transmission serve as proof if there is reason to suspect an element of illusion. Some of the acts of those who urged the above-mentioned forms of worship, and who found a mass following, also fall into this category.

If, however, there is no reason to suspect that an act was wrought by illusion, then (1) either the report is coupled with a claim that, by virtue of reason or the stable tradition of an

---

44. Cf. Samau'al, pp. 13–15.

established religion, clearly cannot relate to God or to another force, or else (2) the report is not coupled with such a claim.[45]

Coupling this claim with the report is either inadmissible because it misleads people (as mentioned in our discussion of miracles), or it is admissible. If it is admissible, it may be that God enabled the miracle-maker to perform because He knew that the intelligent would not be deceived by it, for if they were, they would:

degrade their minds,

or forswear their former faith which was strongly embedded in their hearts and was in opposition to the faith of the miracle-worker. They are neither misled nor degraded when the claim to prophethood has not been coupled with the act of a miracle. If the claim is not coupled with transmitted reports of extraordinary phenomena that are in no way accountable as illusion, the claim is invalid on rational grounds, and not because of [faulty] transmission.

Some people do not posit the evidence of miracles to establish that the claimant to prophethood is right, and that because of doubts previously mentioned, of which, they claim, they are unable to rid themselves. But you know the argument from earlier discussion. Among this group of people are some who veto prophethood altogether, as do, reportedly, the Barāhima.[46]

Others profess belief in prophethood not exclusively by miracles but by concomitants that posit belief. Some Jews acknowledge the prophethood of Moses in this sense: they claim that the belief of the Jewish people is not based merely upon his miracles, great and numerous though they were, but upon having themselves heard the divine speech unto Moses at Mount Sinai, so that they knew his prophethood in their conscience just as the prophet knows his prophethood as self-evident; and those Jews carried that tradition to their prog-

45. *Ibid.*, pp. 8–10. The curious expression "god or another force" stems from the Koran, where it occurs over a dozen times, sometimes in the phrase "a deity other than God" (cf. 6:14, 40, 46, 114, 146, 164; 16:54, 116).

46. Cf. chap. 1, n. 24, above.

eny in an uninterrupted transmission. They assert that they achieved the perfect belief in this fashion, not through argument based on miracles wrought; and that the miracles of Moses, such as cleavage of the sea, turning water into blood, destruction in the land of Egypt of all the first-born animals and humans except among the Israelites, the pillar of cloud, the supply of manna for over forty years to a numerous nation, and others—although no intelligent man will admit illusion in these—merely strengthen the conviction already prevalent among them. As far as we know, this divine speech to the community is a phenomenon that obtained only in this particular case of prophethood.[47]

Some people do posit divine verification for the acts of a
45 challenger through miracles of the above variety. Most people are of this opinion. Jews who hold this view assert that a transmitted report about miracles that satisfies the cumulative conditions of verification is available only for Moses and the other Jewish prophets. They reject the opponent's view "that your transmission is not sounder than theirs." And you know what has been said concerning the transmission of the Jews.

**The seventh objection.**

We do not concede the impossibility of abrogation of the law of the Jews. Indeed, abrogation occurs, cleaves to them. Now, if it does occur, and if, in several passages, the Torah contradicts this, then, in our view, the Torah's veracity is impaired. There are five instances demonstrating that abrogation does occur.

The first is the Torah's regulation stipulating that if one is in the presence of a dying person, touches a bone of a dead person, or treads upon a tomb, he becomes unclean, and can be cleansed only with the ashes of the cow which the Aaronid priest used to burn.[48] If the Jews nowadays dispense with this form of purification because of their inability to procure those ashes, they admit abrogation on account of a situation brought on by present conditions. If they do not dispense with it, they are unclean, which is in opposition to their belief, for they

47. Cf. *Kh.*, Book I, par. 87, but the wording is different.

48. Num. 19: 19 f.

offer prayers, carry scrolls of the law, and avoid a menstruating woman so as not to be defiled by her.[49]

The second is that the Jews claim that everything in their books of jurisprudence is tradition preserved by legists on behalf of trustworthy authorities down to Moses. If so, their dissension on legal matters stems either from an irregularity in the chain of authority, which is against their religion, or from the clash of two traditions, each abrogating the other. Q.E.D.

The third is that there are sections in their prayers which contain supplications obviously compiled after the destruction of the Jewish state. They have fasts that also indicate post-state origin, such as the fast of the burning of the Temple, the fast of the siege of the Temple, the fast of Gedalia, and the fast of the hanging of Haman. They have declared all these obligatory though the Torah forbade the addition of any new precept.[50] Thus the Torah's prohibition is abrogated.

The fourth is that their Torah states that no king the Israelites set over themselves should have many wives, lest he be seduced; nor should he have much gold or silver.[51] Yet David had many wives, as did his son Solomon, who, in addi- 46
tion, had much gold and silver. This indicates abrogation. Many other passages in the prophetic books show violations of the legislation of the Torah, but there is no need to dwell on them.

The fifth is that the Torah makes circumcision obligatory on the eighth day after birth, and prohibits any manner of work on the Sabbath.[52] Each of these obligations negates the other if the eighth day after birth falls on a Sabbath. There are other passages in the Torah pointing to abrogation, and the careful scrutinizer will recognize them.

**Reply.**[53]

The word meaning "impurity" in the Hebrew language is used in three senses. It is used for disobedience and the

---

49. Cf. Samau'al, pp. 16–21/38–41.
50. Deut. 13: 1.
51. Deut. 17: 17; I Kings 10:10–11:4.
52. Gen. 17: 10–14; Exod. 20: 8–11.
53. *Guide*, Book III, chap. 47.

contravention of command, either in deed or thought; for impurities, such as excrement and urine; and for such abstract notions as touching a certain thing, carrying it, or being in the same room with it. It is in this third sense that the word is applied to one touching a dead person. He is enjoined not to approach anything sacred until after ritual purification with the aforementioned ashes of the cow. He is not denied the right to pray or to carry the scripture before such purification, in contrast to the unclean who is defiled through contact with impurities; for he who is defiled by the latter must neither pray nor carry a scripture, but plain water is sufficient for his cleansing. It is ignorance of the various meanings of the Hebrew word indicating "impurity" that gave rise to this query.

The juridical queries of the Jews are not all taken from tradition; some stem from the scriptural text, some from tradition, and some from speculation and analogy founded on premises in text and tradition. Dissent occurs not about true tradition but about matters derived from it that are dependent upon speculation and individual judgment. The claim that *all* their tradition comes from trustworthy authorities is something no Jew makes, let alone all Jews.

Concerning the Jews following the stipulations of their chief authorities and judges, despite the Torah prohibition against adding to or subtracting from the Law, know then that the Torah enjoined submission to the prophets who follow the law of Moses.[54] The Jewish sages say that the prophets may issue no command that would permanently annul any Torah stipulation, or they would not be followers of that law; but they may prescribe annulment when a situation requires it,
47 on condition that the annulment not be continuous, as in the case of the prophet Elijah, who offered sacrifice in an unauthorized place—an annulment that could not be permanent.[55]

The Torah also calls for obedience to the religious authorities and judges supported by the divine presence in the land God chose, even if they be not prophets, providing that

54. Cf. Deut. 17: 8–12; 18–18. Cf. *Kh.*, Book III, par. 39.
55. I Kings 18: 30–38; TB *Yebamoṯ* 90b. Cf. *JE*, s.v. *Abrogation.*

the new stipulations do not contradict any Torah stipulation, permanently or otherwise. It is hardly likely that these men formed an agreement to contradict the law, because they were many, with vast knowledge, both old and new, and were only rarely left without prophetic guidance or a substitute, namely, hearing divine speech voiced by an undetected speaker called in Hebrew *bat̲ qol,* and so on. If following these authorities was a duty that stemmed from the Torah, then such following constitutes no addition to Torah stipulations. It is even possible that that which they added was the result of divine inspiration.

As for David and Solomon, they were not immune to sin according to the Jews, because neither was a messenger of God. Immunity is to be expected only in the prophet-messenger and only in his mission, but immunity beyond that is doubtful.[56] Still, according to their legists, David did not exceed the permissible number of wives. His son Solomon had much gold and silver, perhaps not for himself, but in the interests of the nation, which is not forbidden. Regarding Solomon's many wives, the text of the book states that he sinned by reason of violating this precept.[57] To him who has grasped what we have said, the solution of textual problems of this type in the books of the other prophets will present no difficulty.

As to the precept of circumcision and the Sabbath, the former antedates the latter, making it clear that when all manner of work on the Sabbath was forbidden, circumcision was excepted, and therefore there is no abrogation. The solution to cases of this type in the Torah presents no difficulty to a man of insight.

It is important to know that these objections, in their entirety, will be marshalled only by one outside the Christian and Islamic faiths, for the creeds of both these faiths would oppose citing all of the objections, though each may cite some.

---

56. Cf. the judgment of *Guide,* Book II, chap. 45, on the second degree of prophecy.

57. I Kings 11.

48 Thus the Christians recognize the prophethood of Moses and the prophets of his faith, all their miracles, and the veracity of the Torah and the prophetic books. They could not deny that the Jews recognize resurrection and judgment after death, for the Acts of the Apostles states that Paul, whose name had been Saul, said that he was of the Pharisees who taught "the good hope and resurrection," and the belief in angels and the spirit,[58] unlike the heretic Jews of that time, the Sadducees—followers of a man called Sadok who did not teach this at all. The Pharisees were the main body of the Jews in the past; at the present time they are called Rabbanites. The followers of Sadok, however, were few; their sect declined steadily and disappeared.

Several Gospel passages indicate the Jews' teaching concerning requital after death; they will be clear to the observant reader. The [Christians], however, claim that the law of the Torah was abrogated by Christ, though the Gospel states:[59]

I did not come to destroy the law of Moses but I came to fulfill it by the work of truth, amen amen; I say unto you: Till heaven and earth pass, one jot or one tittle shall in no wise pass from the law of Moses, nor will anything be abolished from his law; whosoever therefore shall lessen from the law of Moses anything, little or great, he shall be called the least in the Kingdom of Heaven.

When the Jews blamed Jesus because one of his disciples gleaned and ate the corns of wheat on the Sabbath, he did not reply that the Sabbath had been abrogated but explained that the precept did not prevent one who had to eat from doing so, just as David, when needing food, was not prevented from eating from the Lord's table, even though this was not permitted.[60] Jesus adhered to the precepts of the Torah to the end, as did his disciples after his death. Only much later, when they had to mingle with the gentiles, did Paul stop them from complying with the precepts.

58. Acts 23: 6–8.

59. Matt. 5: 17–19.

60. *Ibid.*, 12; I Sam. 21: 4–7.

The Muslims also recognize the prophethood of Moses and his miracles, as well as the prophethood of prophets before and after him and their miracles. They agree that the Jews recognize reward in paradise and chastisement in hell. Thus, concerning paradise the glorious Koran says, "and they said: no one but those who are Jews or Christians will enter paradise,"[61] in the sense that each of the two communities maintained that only those belonging to it would enter paradise. On the subject of hell, another passage of the glorious Koran puts it: "And they said: 'Fire will not touch us except for a number
of days.' "[62] The consensus of the interpreters is that this is a 49
report of the Jews' tenet. It is also mentioned in the Koran that the hereafter had been revealed to Moses as stated in the sura *Sabbiḥ*: "Nay ye prefer the nearer life, but the Hereafter is better and more lasting; verily, this is in the ancient pages, the pages of Abraham and Moses."[63]

But the Muslims will say that the Torah was changed, and will deny the soundness of the transmission of the Jews in carrying its tradition. They say this despite the fact that the Koran and the Muslim tradition indicate that the Torah was in the possession of the Jews at the time of Muhammad, for example: "But how shall they make thee their judge, seeing that in their hands is the Torah containing the judgment of God?"[64] It does not say "some of the Torah" nor that the Torah has been distorted. Numerous verses of the Koran are in the same strain. The verse "The Jews twist the word from its position"[65] and similarly the verse "and woe to those who write the Book with their hands, and then say: this is from God, that they may buy with it some small gain"[66]—these do not indicate that the Koran alludes to the Torah. There are, no doubt, some Jews who relate false traditions, just as there are some such Muslims.

---

61. Koran 2: 105(111).
62. *Ibid.*, 2: 74 (80).
63. *Ibid.*, 87: 16–19.
64. *Ibid.*, 5: 47 (43).
65. *Ibid.*, 4: 48 (46).
66. *Ibid.*, 2: 73 (79).

76

The distortion of the Torah after Muhammad, as you know, is clearly something no intelligent person can imagine. The islamic religion cannot exist unless it teaches the abrogation of the religion of Moses. That is the reason the Muslims had to impugn the transmission of the Jews and adopt the tenet of the distortion of the Torah, lest the Torah, including its indications of perpetual validity and nonabrogation, should be binding upon them.

Some Muslims interpret the words in the Torah on the law's perpetual validity to mean *for a long time to come*; for example, it says in the Torah about a Hebrew servant: Six years he shall serve and in the seventh year, he shall be freed, and if he refuses liberation, let his ear be pierced and let him serve forever. The text meant that he should serve up to fifty years, as stated in another passage.[67]

The Jews say: we do not rely on mere words about the perpetual validity of the scripture, nor do we deny that these words may be used metaphorically in another passage, but we say that we know conclusively from the words on the perpetual validity and their parallels in the Torah and the prophetic books, and from the words of the carriers of the tradition of the faith, that Moses professed the perpetuity of his law, just as your own knowledge that your law will not be abrogated stems not only from mere scriptural proofs that are not conducive to certainty.

50 The Muslims answer them thus: If this were so, everybody who had contact with you would know that; yet the Christians, despite their vast numbers and the fact that they have read your books, do not know it. Indeed, since it became known as a tenet of the religion of Muhammad that Islam would not be abrogated, a Muslim knows that, and so does a non-Muslim who had contact with Muslims.[68]

The Jews may say: if the contacts of non-Jews with us were as close as our contacts with Muslims, this necessarily

---

67. Exod. 21: 2, 6; Lev. 25: 39–43; Deut. 15: 12–18. Lev. 25: 40, unto the year of jubilee. Cf. TB *Qiddushin* 15, jubilee or death of master end enslavement.

68. Cf. *Muḥaṣṣal*, p. 151.

would be known concerning our faith. But the contact of Muslims with Jews does not necessitate a Muslim inquiry into what the Jews assert, especially since the Jews are prevented from declaring their creed, and their books are in a tongue the Muslims do not understand. The contact of a minority with a majority affects the majority and the minority differently. Thus, when a linguistic minority is in contact with a linguistic majority, the minority learns the language of the majority whilst the majority does not learn the language of the minority or, at best, learns it much later. Moreover, despite numerous contacts of the bulk of the Jews with the Muslims, many Jews still do not know the basic Islamic tenets known by the rank and file Muslims, let alone the elite. It is even more natural that a similar situation should obtain on the Muslim side, or, at the very least, that both sides should be equal [in mutual ignorance].[69]

Furthermore, how can one gainsay this when one finds, despite the undeniably strong contact between the [Muslim] factions, some Muslims denying that for which other Muslims claim the authority of transmission, for example, the clear word on the imamate.[70] Similarly, one faction denies what the other claims as a transmitted report on how the Prophet extolled his companions, announced to some of them their admission to paradise, and praised them. Each of the two factions denies what the other claims by transmission.[71]

---

69. The Jews spoke the languages of the countries in which they lived. In Iraq they spoke Arabic. But the author refers to the language of canonic texts. The canonic texts of the Jews were not in Arabic. It is in this sense that the Jews are here classified as a *linguistic* minority.

70. The Shi'ites claimed that the Prophet Muhammad clearly indicated that his son-in-law, 'Alī, should be the successor of the Prophet in leadership. " 'Alī is the master of anybody to whom I was master" (Ibn Ḥanbal, *Musnad* [Cairo, 1954], II, 54, no. 641); or "O God, be friendly to those who are friendly to him, and be enemy of those who are his enemies" (*ibid.*, p. 195, no. 950; pp. 200 f., no. 961; p. 328, no. 1310); or "Support his supporter, forsake those who forsake him" (*ibid.*, p. 195, no. 951; cf. p. 201, no. 964).

71. Thus one story has it that only one person was promised paradise by the Prophet ('Abdallah b. Salām); but several traditions report ten such promises.

# CHAPTER 3

## *On the belief of the Christians in the Lord Jesus Christ, who is Jesus the son of Mary, peace be upon them; his message; in what manner he is, according to them, both prophet and deity; opinions and counter-opinions therewith connected.*

THE Christians teach the following:

We believe all that is in the Torah and in the records of the Israelites, records whose veracity is irrefutable because they are widely known and available to the masses. We believe that toward the very end of the [sacred] history of the Jews, Deity became incarnate and an embryo in the body of a virgin chosen from among the noblest of the women of the Israelites, the progeny of David. She gave birth to a being outwardly human, and essentially divine; who was outwardly sent forth as a prophet, and essentially sent forth as a deity; he was fully man and fully deity. This is Christ, called the Son of God. God is the Father, the Son, and the Holy Ghost.

They maintain:

We are truly monotheists, though we make mention of Trinity with our tongues. We believe in God and in His sojourn among the Israelites as a distinction to them, for the divine power never ceased to be attached to them until their people rebelled against our Messiah, and crucified Him. Then divine wrath became unremitting against their people, and divine favor was continuous toward the few followers of Christ—from among whom Christ elected twelve persons corresponding to the number of tribes of Israel—and later favor was extended toward the gentile nations following those few believers. We are [spiritually] of the Children of Israel although we are not of their progeny. We are the more worthy of being designated as Israelites because we follow the Messiah and his Apostles. Those few believers were followed by the many who became the leaven for the community of the Christians, and they merited the status of the Israelites. The Christians were successful, and spread into many lands and nations calling the people unto the Christian faith, urging its worship with respect to the cult of Christ and his Cross, and complying with His decrees and with the testaments of His Apostles, as well as with laws derived from the Torah which Christians read and which is irrefutably true and divine.[1] Those who have faith in this call follow it obediently, voluntarily, and willingly without being compelled thereto by sword or coercion.

The Christians agreed upon this creed in a resolution 52
by a council of 318 persons in the time of Constantine. Its sense is as follows:[2]

> We believe in One God the Father, All-Sovereign, Maker of heaven and earth, and of all things visible and invisible;
>
> And in one Lord Jesus Christ, the only-begotten Son of God, Begotten of the Father before all the ages, Light of Light, true God of true God, begotten not made, of one substance with the Father, through whom all

---

1. Up to this point the opening follows *Kh.*, Book I, par. 4.

2. The "Nicene" creed of "the 318 fathers who met at Nicea (325) and that of the 150 who met at a later time" (in Constantinople. 381) was approved at the Council of Chalcedon, 451. Cf. T. H. Bindley, *The Oecumenical Documents of the Faith*, ed. F. W. Green (4th ed.; London, 1950), pp. 82 f./233; Henry Bettenson, ed., *Documents of the Christian Church* (2d ed.; London, 1963), pp. 34–37.

A different rendition of the creed is found in *Kitāb al-Milal wa-al-nihal* by Shahrastani (d. 1153), ed. W. Cureton (London, 1842), p. 174 f. Shahrastani's account of Christianity was presumably one of Ibn Kammuna's sources.

In the Arabic text, *'awālim stands for aiōnoi*=the ages (thus reflecting an Aramaic version) and *ta panta*=all things. "He was made flesh—of the Holy Spirit—became man who was conceived and born of the Virgin Mary" (*ḥumila bihi wa-wulida min* etc.). "With glory" is omitted, as well as "of whose kingdom . . ."

things were made; who for us men and for our salvation came down from the heavens, and was made flesh of the Holy Spirit and the Virgin Mary, and became man, and was crucified for us under Pontius Pilate, and suffered and was buried, and rose again on the third day according to the Scriptures, and ascended into the heavens, and sitteth on the right hand of the Father, and cometh again with glory to judge living and dead, of whose kingdom there shall be no end;

And in the Holy Spirit, the Lord and the Life-giver, that proceedeth from the Father, who with Father and Son is worshiped together and glorified together, who spake through the prophets;

In one Holy Catholic and Apostolic Church;

We acknowledge one baptism unto remission of sins. We look for a resurrection of the dead, and the life of the age to come.

This is the end of their creed.

I found no disagreement between the Jacobites and the Nestorians concerning the text, except that in the version I obtained from the Jacobites I did not find "through whom the worlds and all things were made"; and instead of "according to the Scriptures," I found "as He desired." It contained additions that in no way contradict this creed.

The two agree that the hypostasis of the Father is the Essence; the hypostasis of the Son is the Word, which is Knowledge, and that it is born from the Father, not by way of procreation, but as the light of the sun is born of the sun; the hypostasis of the Holy Ghost is Life, and it continuously emanates from the Father.

They also agree on the union of the Word with the Lord Jesus. Yet they differ about the [concept of the] Unity itself.

According to the Jacobites, a third element is produced out of fusion and mixture, just as the fusion of fire with coal produces a live coal, and the live coal is neither pure fire nor
53 pure coal. They consider this a fixed compound, even though it be corporeal and spiritual, like that of the abstract soul with the body: one is tied with the other to become one person.

They say that Christ is an essence [consisting] of two essences, and a hypostasis of two hypostases.

The Nestorian tenet conceives of the union in the sense that the Word made Jesus its abode and seat, and entered[3] into Him. The Nestorians also declare that Christ is two essences, two hypostases.

Some say that the union occurs in Him as union occurs between the engraving of a seal and the wax, or between the image of the face and the mirror, without the engraving being transported from the seal unto the wax, or the face into the mirror.

Some maintain that the union of the Word with Him meant that the Word was manifested and carried out by Him.

The Melkites, however, teach that Christ is two essences but one hypostasis, because the union took place in the universal man, not in the particular. By hypostasis is meant a person [of the Trinity].

All Christians believe in bodily resurrection and reward in bliss hereafter, and express this by the word paradise; chastisement is found in hell. But they believe only in spiritual, not corporeal, reward and punishment. They say that the virtuous will become angel-like in the Kingdom of Heaven, or in the Kingdom of God. They believe in the immortality of the human soul after the destruction of the body in death.

They all agree that their religion, founded by Jesus Christ and his Apostles, will not be abrogated until the day of resurrection. They know this as a tradition, on the authority of the Apostles who learned it from their own minds as something evident beyond doubt.

The Christians have a tradition of numerous miracles performed by Christ as related in the Four Gospels, that is, of Matthew, Mark, Luke, and John. These include the revival of three dead persons: one before he was put into a coffin, another in a coffin before burial, and the third, four days after he had been buried.[4]

3. *Iddara'athu* = "Clad itself with him; made him its innermost garment by closely cleaving to him" (E. W. Lane, *Arabic-English Lexicon*, p. 871).

4. Matt. 9: 18–25; Luke 7: 11–15; John 11: 1–44.

It is John who, in his Gospel, mentions the resurrection of the third. In some gospels only one of them is mentioned, in others, two. Only the gospel of John mentions the resurrection of the buried one. Apart from that, the gospels agree on the resurrection of the man who was not put into the coffin, the healing of the ill and the leper, the turning of water into wine, the feeding of 5,000 men (apart from the women and children) with two fish and five loaves, the casting out of devils from human beings, the healing of many diseases, the walking on the water, and the other miracles of Jesus.[5]

There are many discrepancies among the four gospels
54 which the Christian scholars try in some way to harmonize. The gospels contain many parables and sermons. They contain the command of noble moral traits; for example:

> If you requite evil with evil you merit no reward from your Father in Heaven; if you forgive men their trespasses your Father in Heaven will forgive your trespasses, but if you forgive not neither will He forgive you.[6]

There was among Christians much dissension about the creed. Thus, some maintain existence in time for the Son, or say that God created the Son and empowered him to create the World; while the others say that Christ was born of His Father before all the worlds were created and was not created in time, as also stated in the agreed-upon creed. They had numerous councils which attempted to eliminate internal strife, and at these some of the dissenters were excommunicated, which led to much bloodshed among them. This is known from their history books.

Such changes in the stipulations of the Torah as—for example, to make lawful [the consumption of] the flesh of swine, and the abandonment of circumcision and laving [of hands]—are told of the Apostles, not about Jesus Christ, for he adhered to the stipulations of the Torah until the Jews seized him. He

5. Matt. 8: 5–17; 14: 15–21, 22–32, 34–36; 15: 21–28; 17: 14–18; Mark 1: 23–45.
6. Matt. 6: 14–15.

would enjoin them to comply with those stipulations and He said:[7] I am not come to destroy, but to fulfil [the law].

When the Jews blamed him for what they imagined to be neglect of some Torah stipulations, he explained to them that it was not neglect, and clarified this unto them in accord with their jurisprudence and law, as is mentioned in the Gospel.[8] His disciples continued for a long time with this adherence to the Torah, before they began to break its laws and declared that the Torah was abrogated and had been obligatory only until the advent of Jesus Christ. Most of this goes back to the apostle Paul.[9]

The opponents of Christianity may say:

If the hypostases you mentioned suggest three entities existing independently, the principle of monotheism invalidates that inference, and it also contradicts your creed on the unity of God. But if you mean that the hypostases are attributes, or that one of them is essence, and the other two are attributes, then have you not turned the attribute of power into a fourth hypostasis, and similarly the other terms to describe God into hypostases? Should they say:

His power is His knowledge

we say: His life also is His knowledge and why have you separated it into a hypostasis?

The idea of the union is not intelligible, because two things that unite are either existent or nonexistent, or one of the two is existent, and the other nonexistent. If the two exist, there is no union because they are two, not one; if the two do not exist, they become not one, and a third element, also nonexistent, appears; if one is nonexistent and the other remains, 55
then clearly there is no union. The monotheistic principle is contradicted if, supposing union to mean mixing, blending, or compounding, the Father and Son are two separate substances in which the Son merges with Christ, and the Father,

7. Matt. 5: 17 (quoted in TB *Shabbaṯ* 116*b*).

8. Matt. 12.

9. Rom. 9–10.

in the sense mentioned above, does not. If again the Son is an attribute, it cannot be understood about the knowing essence that its being knowing becomes blended with some body without the essence. Just as it is beyond understanding that Zayd can be in Baghdad while his being knowing is in Khurasan. Further, the knowledge of everything by Him must necessarily include the knowledge of God and the knowledge of Christ simultaneously, so the same attribute actually has two carriers, which is absurd. If, again, God was not knowing at the moment of union, then his being knowing would be a vain assertion, thus he would need a specifier (to endow him with knowledge), and this precludes him from divinity.

The tenet of fusion is false because fusion can be conceived only of bodies, and the Christians do not consider the Word a body. If they say fusion is compounded by connection—for example, one man consisting of body and soul—then the connection of one with the other can be grasped only in terms of the dependence upon each other. On the one hand, this dependence can be mutual (the body and the soul both need each other) or, on the other hand, nonmutual (the shape of a couch needs wood but the wood does not need the shape of a couch). But in the case under consideration, it is precluded that the divine part in any way may need something else, and if union was caused by the need of the human part for the divine, without mutuality, such union would occur to all creatures because all depend on God for every need, including their existence.

A body created in time cannot become preexisting and infallible, and thus it is absurd to make the analogy between the engraving of a seal with wax and the essence of Christ becoming an image of the Creator, if that is what the Christians mean by union. If they mean that Christ possessed a special characteristic enabling him to do things others cannot, this, in itself, does not testify to his being a deity, or else every miracle-working prophet would be a deity. Moses would be a notable example, his miracles being much greater and less susceptible to the possibility of illusion than those attributed to Christ. And, furthermore, the miracles of Moses have a larger number of tradition-carriers, namely the three faiths as opposed to only two for Jesus.

Also, it cannot be said of something that it consists of the substance of another unless the two share in a matter of substance and are encompassed by a community of nature, not one of relation. If one is entirely inseparable from the other, then the Father being parent to the Son is no more appropriate 56
than the opposite. Has not the son, furthermore, begotten a son in turn, who again begat one and so on, *ad infinitum*? If one is differentiated from the other in substance, it follows that the Creator is composed of genus and differentia or that the essence of the Son is like the essence of the Father with some addition. All this is absurd.

If the intent of your teaching is that the Creator is one substance in three hypostases, in that he is knowing and living essence, or an essence that perceives itself, with its essence an object of knowledge for itself (Yaḥyā b. ʻAdī is reported to have interpreted the Father as being God's pure reason, the Son as being God's knowing Himself, and the Holy Ghost as being God's knowledge of His essence), then the assertion is contradicted by your agreed-upon creed—which confirms that the Son is an essence different from that of the Father, or that it was the essence of the Son which descended and rose rather than that of the Father.[10]

If the divine substance and the human substance are inseparable, it can be said to the Jacobites, then, that their tenet that Christ is a substance of two substances and a hypostasis of two hypostases—divine substance and human substance—is the same as the Nestorian tenet; if each substance precludes the other, the Jacobites would be discarding the deity, and it would follow that Christ is neither preexistent nor created, neither deity nor nondeity, because none of these descriptions fits him. Furthermore, it is evident that the human in Christ is identical with the human in anybody, and the divine in him

10. Yaḥyā b. ʻAdī (893–974), Jacobite theologian. Cf. Aug. Périer's study, *Yaḥyā b. ʻAdī* (Paris, 1920), pp. 162–167, 182–185, and his edition *Petits traités apologétiques de Yaḥyā ben ʻAdī* (Paris, 1920), pp. 19, 25, 26, 83, 90.

did not nullify this. The opposite view is inadmissible because the divine influences the human without the latter influencing the former.

It may be said to the Nestorians—who maintain the theory of two substances and hypostases—that, if they both are preexistent, you postulate a fourth preexistent: Christ's humanity; and if they were created in time, then the Son is created who, you assert, is eternal, and you then worship one who is no God because you worship Jesus who, according to this view, is two substances created in time. If one of the two substances is preexistent and the other is created, and you worship the preexistent and the created—inasmuch as Jesus whom you worship is the total of both—and the total of preexistent and created, insofar as he is this total, is created, then it means that you worship the created. But the created, as such, does not merit worship. Worship should be reserved only to the preexistent, and worshiping that which was created in time is out of place. If you exclude the created from being the object of
57 worship, you then would not worship the total, but that would mean that Christ who stands for the total of the two things does not merit worship, in contradiction to your belief.

The Melkite tenet that Christ is two substances, one by hypostasis with the union occurring in the universal man rather than in the particular, is a false theory because all men share in the universal man, and if the Word united with him, it follows that no man is especially distinguished by this union. Similarly, if he is not two hypostases, then he is not two substances either.

Thus all your denominations are false.

Furthermore, God is too exalted to be described as having dwelled in the uncleanness of the menstruating womb and in the confinement of the belly and darkness; or that bodily eyes looked at Him; or that He was affected by slumber or sleep; or that He excremented in his clothes and urinated in his bed; or that He wept or laughed; or that He was helpless against what He did not want; or that He was lost in thought, imprisoned, overcome with fear and desirous of human possession; or that He fled. God is too exalted for it to be said that He ate, drank, and behaved like earthly humans; or that He could not assert Himself while ruling the world until He descended upon earth to guide men and save them from Satan; or that He came to purify men of their sins and to guide them from going astray; or that the Jews maltreated, tortured, crucified, and humiliated Him; or that He spent three days in His grave.[11]

What sin before or after Christ was greater, in your opinion, than the one committed in his time? And yet the Devil, just as he did before the advent of Christ, has continued to lead astray and harm men following Christ's advent. The devil split your religion into various sects and you testify about one another's heresies. In some countries the apostles were slain, humiliated, and tortured. Oppression, enmity, massacre, and unbelief are widespread among Christians and other nations to this day.

One may say to the Christians:

If Christ is considered a God because he is, in your view, without a parent, then Adam and Eve, along with every primeval beast God created, are more wondrous than he in this respect. The propet Elijah was unaffected in his human existence by misfortune and, after working numerous miracles, was taken into heaven before Christ, if that is a requisite for being God. If worshiping a human being were permissible, Elijah would be more entitled to deification than he who was imprisoned, humiliated, tortured, and crucified. The angels, also are too exalted to be commanded to descend. Jesus is worshiped, let us say, because the Gospel called him the Son of God, but on the other hand, you avow that God called Israel "my first-born son,"[12] and that Jesus called the apostles
his brothers.[13] It also says in the Gospel, "Love them which 58
love you," and so on, down to "you will be like my Father and your Father which is in Heaven;"[14] also, "if you requite trespasses with trespasses, you have no reward from your

11. The whole passage thus stresses the incompatibility of the human aspect in Jesus with the notion of divinity.

12. Exod. 4: 22.

13. Matt. 12: 49–50; 28: 10.

14. Matt. 5: 43–48, but inexact.

Father;" and, "if you forgive men their trespasses, your [heavenly] Father will also forgive you."[15] And, if his divinity is claimed because of his miracles, then, to repeat, other prophets, too, had wrought them.

One can also say to them:

How can you say that Christ had been susceptible of sin until John the Baptist cleansed him?[16] Yet you cannot say he had not been touched by sin, otherwise the purification by water [the baptism] was pointless.

Would the deity drink wine, eat fish and game, and be tired because of weakness until sweat poured down his face?[17] Would the devil have the power to snatch and carry him away against his will?[18]

And what of the statement in the Gospel which says "[think] not that I am come to destroy the law but to fulfil."[19] But you, Christians, did destroy much of it?

In the Gospel of Matthew it says that Gabriel came to Mary, and announced to her the birth of a child but he did not tell her "rejoice, thou wilt bear a deity."[20]

Joseph was the husband of Mary, as it is stated in Matthew that the angel, that is, Gabriel, came and said to Joseph: "Fear not to take [unto thee Mary] thy wife."[21] Elsewhere in the Gospel we find that Jesus is the son of Joseph, and that Mary admitted that Jesus was the son of Joseph, for on the day she found him in the Temple she said: "Where hast thou been? Behold, thy father and I have sought thee sorrowing."[22] And the people of Nazareth said: "Is not this the son of the carpenter and his brothers are James and Judah, and are not his sisters married among us?"[23]

---

15. Cf. Matt. 6: 14–15.
16. Matt. 3: 13–17.
17. Matt. 11: 18–19; Luke 22: 44.
18. Matt. 4.
19. Matt. 5: 17.
20. Matt. 1: 18–21; cf. Luke 1: 26–33.
21. Matt. 1: 20.
22. Luke 2: 48.
23. Matt. 13: 55–56; Mark 6: 3.

How is it possible that Christ should be fully deity when he knows only some things and not all, especially if you say that the hypostasis of the son is the word, which is knowledge. A proof that he did not know certain things, a proof that the union you claim did not take place, is in the Gospel of Mark where we find that when Jesus mentioned some of the terrors of the hour and its conditions, he said: "But of that day and that hour knoweth no man, no, not the angels which are in heaven, neither the Son, but the Father."[24]

It is said in the Gospel that he slept in the boat and did not know it until somebody awoke him.[25] The prophet David says: "Behold, He that keepeth Israel doth neither slumber nor sleep";[26] also: "For who [in the skies] can be compared
[unto the Lord]; thou dost not sleep, O exalted one."[27] 59

In the Gospel it says: "If ye have faith as a grain of mustard seed, ye shall say unto this mountain—Remove hence to yonder place—and it shall remove."[28] But we find none of the believers in Jesus able to move a light stone or anything else.

The Gospel says that the bird found a nest to dwell in and the fox a stone to dwell in, but the son of man found no place to dwell.[29] Yet the prophet Isaiah says that the Messiah will sit upon the throne of David and will judge the people in justice and righteousness.[30]

Jesus rose and washed the feet of the apostles in water and said: "The son of man has not come to be served but has come to serve."[31] He never called himself a true deity.

As for the Cross, it was displayed by Helene and Constantine some 300 years after Jesus, and it is not mentioned in the Gospel or any other book.

A man said to Jesus: "Make me clean" and he replied: "I

---

24. Mark 13:32.
25. Matt. 8: 23–25.
26. Ps. 121: 4.
27. Pss. 89: 7?; 44: 23–24? The Arabic ends: sleep not *etc.*
28. Matt. 17: 20.
29. Matt. 8: 20
30. Isa. 9: 6.
31. Cf. John 13: 5, 16.

am eager to cleanse thee, go to the priest, show thyself to him, offer a sacrifice, as God commanded Moses in the Torah."[32] How then can he be regarded a deity if he has no tenet of his own but refers to another's tenet? This is so despite his saying: "Who sees me, sees my Father, and I and my Father are one."[33]

He said to his disciples: "Sit ye here, while I go and pray [yonder]." He said: "My soul [is exceeding sorrowful] even unto death; tarry you here until I have prayed." He said in his prayer: "O my Father, if it be possible, let this cup pass from me." He said to Simon "[What] couldst thou not watch with me one hour? Rise, let us be going, for the hour has come."[34] He had said earlier: "And this Son of Man will be delivered into the hands of the sinners, and they will scoff at him, and spit in his face."[35] Previously, he had fasted and prayed for 40 days on the mountain, in devotion to God, and was tempted of the devil until great hunger seized him, as recorded in the Gospel:[36]

> The devil continued to seek Jesus, and found him on the mountain as he was perishing of hunger and thirst. The devil then said to him: If thou be the son of God, as thou sayest, then say to this stone that it be bread, that thou mayest eat. Then Jesus said to the devil: it is written in the Torah, man shall not live by bread alone but by [every] word of God shall man live.[37] Then the devil
> 60 took Jesus into the holy city and setteth him on a pinnacle of the Temple, and saith unto him, if thou be the son of God, as thou sayest, cast thyself down, and no evil shall befall thee. But Jesus said unto the devil: It is written in the Torah, you shall not tempt the Lord, your God.[38] The devil said to Jesus: The world, and its kingdom, and all the good of the world is mine, fall down and worship

32. Matt: 8: 2–4.
33. Cf. John 10: 30, 14: 9.
34. Cf. Matt. 26: 36–46; Mark 14: 41.
35. Cf. Matt. 26:2.
36. *ibid.*, 4: 1–11.
37. Cf. Deut. 8: 3.
38. Cf. *ibid.*, 6: 16.

me. But Jesus said to the devil: get thee hence, Satan. It is written in the Torah, fear the Lord, thy God, and Him only shalt thou serve, in Him seek help, and swear in His name.[39]

Now, to whom was he praying and fasting, if he was a deity? How can you claim divinity for one tempted by the devil?

Further, Luke traces Jesus Christ's genealogy to Adam, while Matthew gives a genealogy which differs in certain details. At the beginning of the genealogy in Matthew, Jesus is of the line of David and Abraham, but at the end he says, "Matthan begat Jacob, and Jacob begat Joseph, the husband of Mary, of whom was born Jesus, who is called Christ." Matthew states that Joseph "knew not [Mary] till she had brought forth her first-born son."[40]

It was Judas, one of the twelve companions who were close to Jesus, who led the Jews to seize him, and delivered him to them for crucifixion. Judas took his pay from the Jews therefor: thirty pieces of silver. If he had known that Jesus was a prophet, let alone a deity, he would not have dared to act thus in order to obtain this trifling amount.

Part of the torture and disgrace they inflicted upon Jesus, prior to his crucifixion, was to cover his head and face, to smite his head with reeds, and to say to him: "Prophesy unto us, thou Christ, who is he that smote thee?" A servant of the high priest slapped his face, and they spat at him.[41]

Yet God says to Moses: "Man shall not see me and live." And Israelites said unto Moses: "Thou speak with us, and we will hear and obey, but let not God speak with us lest we die."[42] How, then, can he whose face is slapped be a deity?

The Jews paraded with Jesus on Friday till midday, while he carried on his neck the piece of wood on which he was crucified. And, as you assert, Simon of Cyrene came and carried it for him; then the Jews led him away and crucified him upon it, gave him vinegar to drink, and pierced him with a spear

39. Cf. *ibid.*, v. 13.
40. Luke 3: 38; Matt. 1: 1–17, 25.
41. Matt. 26: 67–68; John 18: 22.
42. Cf. Exod. 33: 20; 21: 19.

after his death. Jesus said on the cross: "My God, my God, why
61 hast Thou forsaken me?" He remained crucified until Joseph of Arimathea came, to whom the body was granted, and Joseph buried it as a corpse. All this is told in the Gospel.[43]

You [the Christians] assert that all human souls since the time God created Adam were imprisoned until Jesus died, and then they were released. This would include the souls of all the prophets and righteous people.

There is nothing in the Gospel to indicate that God addressed Jesus except once; it is reported in John that Christ said, "O Father, glorify Thy name; then came there a voice from Heaven, saying, I have both glorified it, and will glorify it again."[44] Now, how is it that God spoke to his servant Moses times out of number, and did not address His son and beloved except this one time?

Moses, God's servant, hid his face and no man could look at him because of the [beaming] light. But God acted conversely toward His son, and abandoned him to humiliation among his enemies?[45]

The books of the prophets mention certain signs of the messiah and events happening in his time, but these did not occur in Jesus or in his time. For example, one prophet says that the messiah "will smite the land with the voice of his mouth, and with the breath of his lips shall he slay the wicked;" that he will sit on the throne of David, and will judge men in justice and righteousness, the wars will cease, and "nation shall not lift up sword against nation"; and that the wolf shall dwell with the lamb and they will graze together, "and the lion shall eat straw like the ox."[46] This, if taken literally, did not occur in the time of Jesus or after him; if it is a parable, which is more plausible, then it is a parable of the lifting of evils from the world and the cessation of antagonisms among creatures.

But in the time of Jesus just the opposite thereof occurred, such as increased enmity among people because of his

43. Matt. 27: 32, 34, 46, 57–59; Ps. 22: 2.
44. John 12: 28.
45. Exod. 34: 29–35.
46. Isa. 11: 4; 9: 6; 2: 4; 11: 6.

appearance on the scene, and as the result of the great sins perpetrated against him and his companions.

It also says that in the time of the Messiah the sons and daughters of the Israelites will prophesy,[47] and that God will send the prophet Elijah "and he shall turn the heart of the fathers to the children and the hearts of the children to their fathers."[48] References to similar signs of the messiah's advent are numerous in the text of the prophets. But none of them has materialized up to the present.

The few which I have adduced here reproduce only the sense, not the literal text, nor their order in the books of the prophecies.

Furthermore, all the miracles and other phenomena reported about Christ are presented on the authority of individuals who were his companions, and are neither properly transmitted nor reliable. Even should the tradition be sound
it is not rationally improbable that some illusion or collusion 62
had a part in it.

But if the soundness of the Christians' tradition cannot be established, then nothing can be ascertained of their claim that they know clearly, on the authority of the apostles and Christ, that their religion is never to be abrogated.

This is what I see fit to mention of the arguments against the Christians. I now proffer the best of what they might say in answer to these points.

Thus they say:

Regarding the hypostases and the fact that they are limited to three, we follow therein the command received but do not know for what reason they were limited to this number.

As for the union, we do not know its manner in this world; perhaps its truth is disclosed to us in the hereafter. But we believe in it because it is mentioned in the Gospel, in the Acts, and in the testimonies of the prophets. For it says in the Gospel, "He that hath seen me hath seen the father. My father and I are one";[49] and the angel said to the shepherds: "This day

---

47. Joel 3: 1.

48. Mal. 3: 24.

49. John 10: 30, 14: 9–11.

a Saviour is born unto you, the Lord Jesus Christ";[50] and the wife of Zacharias said: 'Whence is this favor to me, that the mother of my lord should come to me?' "[51] At the beginning of the gospel of Mark it says: "This is the beginning of the gospel of Jesus Christ, the Son of God." John says: "The Word was made flesh, and dwelt among us."[52] The utterances of the apostles on the subject are numerous.

Among the testimonies of the prophets about the union is the passage in Job: "I know that my Redeemer liveth, and that He shall stand at the last upon the dust."[53] Solomon said: "In very truth God will dwell on the earth."[54] Isaiah said: "The virgin shall conceive, and bear a son, and his name will be called Immanuel."[55] David said: "God of Gods appeareth in Zion,"[56] and: "the Lord said unto my Lord."[57]

As for the list of descriptions of and utterances about the Messiah that contradict His divinity—for example, sleeping, eating, having pains, and so on—they refer to the human aspect in Him, not to the divine. That is why we say He is fully human and fully divine.

As for your phrase that God was unable to exercise His will until He descended unto the earth, we do not say that; for He is almighty, and does as He wishes, and there can be no objection to Him in His rule. We have no way of knowing the subtleties of His wisdom. Further, this would be an objection also to the miracles of the other prophets, but God can guide men without miracles. Yet no one can say: if He

---

50. Luke 2: 11.

51. Luke 1: 43.

52. John 1: 14.

53. Job. 19: 25.

54. I Kings 8: 27, interrogative: But will God indeed dwell on the earth?

55. Isa. 7: 14.

56. Ps. 84: 8: "Every one of them in Zion appeareth before God." The Hebrew preposition *before* is read with a slight vowel change as *God*, while *God* is taken to be a plural. Hence, *God of Gods*. So in the Septuagint and in the Vulgate.

57. Ps. 110: 1.

could do so He would not have wrought the miracles. Indeed, 63
it would be an objection to any act of the Creator for the benefit of men, for He can let them have that benefit without the mediation of the act.

Concerning the fact that sin did not disappear from earth upon the advent of Christ, we did not claim that it would disappear altogether to the extent that neither evil nor sin would be wrought upon earth. We claimed the disappearance of much unbelief and dissoluteness, which undoubtedly did happen, for it was owing to His advent that faith and equity spread in many regions of the world.

As for the claim of His divinity, it stems not from a few circumstances of His life that might be compared with those of the prophets and others, but from the sum total of His circumstances. It is well known that this was unparalleled either before or after Him.

If somebody else is designated as God's son, it is a metaphor, as both protagonist and antagonist will agree, but in relation to Jesus the term is truth. Proof thereof is the authority of the apostles from whom the creed of the Christian faith was handed down.

Christ's words "I come not to destroy the law . . . but to fulfil it,"[58] mean that the Law contains the promise of the advent of the messiah, and that all its precepts are obligatory up to the time of His advent, not forever or to the day of resurrection. Since His appearance, the Law has been fulfilled (1) by the consummation of the promise of his advent, and (2) by the completion of its obligatoriness.

Also, Jesus, violated none of the stipulations of the Torah, but instead, observed all of them to the end, as we explained, and in this sense, too, He is fulfilling them.

**The opponent [of Christianity] might say:**

We do not concede that the Torah promised the advent of Christ.

**They might say:**

---

58. Matt. 5: 17.

Jacob assembled his sons to announce to them what would happen to them at the end of time, and upon reaching Judah said to him:

> The scepter shall not depart from Judah, nor a lawgiver from between his feet until he comes to whom power is due, and unto him shall the gathering of the peoples be,[59]

*scepter* meaning kingship, and *lawgiver* meaning the prophet. It is known that when Christ appeared, kingship disappeared and prophecy ceased among the Jews. In another passage of the Torah it says:

> I will raise them up a prophet from among their brethren, like unto thee; in him they shall believe,[60]

the pronoun "them" referring to the Israelites, and "thee" meaning Moses, the whole being an allusion to Jesus [so interpreted by Simon Peter].[61]

**Then I would say:**

Kingship departed from Judah over 400 years before
64 Jesus; the kings of the Second Commonwealth were Hasmoneans, that is, Aaronides, of the tribe of Levi. After them kingship was vested in Herod, and in his progeny after him, who were not even of the tribe of Judah. The Christians have no reason to say that Jacob named Judah for Jews in general, by way of designating the entity by what is best in it, for it might be argued that this does not stand to reason in this case. Jacob specified what would happen to each of his sons, and specified Judah's fate in this locution; his name is not an expression for all the Jews.

Further, your claim that *the scepter* refers to kingship, and that the *lawgiver* means the prophet is not certain. Prophethood came to an end over 300 years before the advent of Jesus. And the word used in Hebrew for "scepter" is also used in the sense of "tribe"; one may contest that it was used for *scepter* or that the intent of its use was a *royal scepter*.

---

59. Gen. 49: 10; the classical passage in Christian polemics against Judaism.

60. Deut. 18: 15, 18; a classical passage of Islamic polemics: an announcement of Muhammad's advent.

61. Acts 3: 22–26 (cf. 8: 37).

Whatever the Christians quote as testimony from the prophetic scriptures, upon scrutiny it cannot serve as proof. It would take too long to investigate all their arguments, but the above is a sample of the strongest points upon which they rely. It is more plausible that Jacob's annunciation alluded to David, to the effect that the scepter and leadership would not depart from Judah but will grow until David became king, and all the factions of Israel agreed upon making him king.[62]

The opinion of Simon[63] [that Jesus was the prophet whom the Israelites had been enjoined to submit to and believe in] is inadmissible; rather, the text is an allusion to any future prophet of the religion of Moses. The scriptural context does not call for a reference to any particular prophet, but even if it did, we would continue to deny that the reference is to Jesus. The Christians may say:

Peter's interpretation is for us a trenchant proof, and we rely on it, not on the literal meaning of the words.

The word of Mary that Jesus was the son of Joseph, and the fact that others also called him the son of Joseph, was a statement in accordance with the custom of the time rather than the truth.[64] It has been said that the apostles did not grasp the true nature of Jesus nor know much about Him until after His resurrection from the grave and His ascent into heaven, when the Holy Ghost overshadowed them.[65]

Regarding the genealogical discrepancy in the gospels, 65
the commentators of the gospels have interpreted it, as they have interpreted every discrepancy in the gospels, in a way which seems to preclude any contradiction. These interpretations, which some people may consider farfetched, are not impossible.

As for the annunciations of the advent of Jesus which occur in the prophetic books and which did not apply at the time of Jesus, these, too, have been given a possible, though

62. A. Posnanski, *Schiloh* (Leipzig, 1904) traces the history of the interpretation of this verse.

63. = Peter.

64. Luke 2: 48; Matt. 13: 55–56.

65. Matt. 28: 17–20; Luke 24: 25–51.

farfetched interpretation by the Christian scholars. There is no need to detail these interpretations. They are also combined with numerous quotations from the prophets which the scholars interpret to show that Jesus Christ was the messiah foretold in the prophetic books.

But the Jewish interpretations of these passages preclude those of the Christians. Many of the prophetic texts were distorted by the Christians in the process of translation from Hebrew into Greek and Syriac, and later into Arabic, resulting in a significant discrepancy in meaning, although only in a few words. The Christians, at least partly, recognize the discrepancy. This distortion may be the result of intent or negligence, as well as an insufficient knowledge of the language of the original.

I have adduced the evidences the Christians quote from the prophetic books in the manner that they have translated them, rather than as the Jews have them in Hebrew.

In reply to the opinion that the tradition of the miracles of Jesus and of his life rests on the authority of individuals and, therefore, is not authoritatively transmitted and authentic, Christians may say that those individuals, according to the indubitable report of a great mass of people, wrought more miracles than Christ; further, that these miracles not only indicate the veracity of the miracles of Jesus, but are in truth substantially his, and only accidentally their miracles, and it would be proper to attribute them to Jesus rather than to those individuals. Thus it is established that all that has been reported about him—the miracles and so on—is true, and it becomes manifest therefrom that the truth of the Christian religion will not be abrogated.

In fact, *we* do *not* concede that the reports of the miracles by the companions of Jesus constitute authoritative transmission that induces certainty, like the authoritative transmission about the *existence* of Jesus and the apostles, and his crucifixion; they are rather of the type of rumors that spread, come into vogue, and become quasi-transmitted without being truly transmitted.

66 With regard to the argument that reason does not pre-

clude that the miracles of Jesus occurred through illusion or collusion, the Christians claim their conviction that no such illusion and collusion ever occurred, or could possibly occur; and they claim that there is no difference, in the matter of improbability of illusion between the miracles of Jesus and those of Moses, such as the separation of the sea, and the like. No doubt was entertained about the death and disease of those whom Jesus revived and cured; it may be argued for the veracity thereof that if anyone had had doubts it would have become known among his enemies, Jews and others, in his time, and if it had become known at that time it would have been reported. Doubts have not been reported and, although some ascribed the miracles to magic, or the devil's aid, or to Jesus having learned God's highest name, it is clear that his contemporaries were certain of the absence of illusion or collusion.[66]

This is an argument of *the convinced*, not convincing of certainty, but perhaps it might confirm a prevailing notion once their transmitted tradition is accepted.

But if the argument is supported by viewing all the details of the life of Jesus and his companions—their asceticism, piety, and endurance of great suffering in establishing the church and organizing their religion so thoroughly—then from the totality of these concomitants it becomes clear that their cause depends on divine support and concern from on high.

Some of the other arguments of the antagonists mentioned above stem from sheer defamation and rejection, and others will be refuted by the intelligent reader with some effort but no difficulty.

I did not find most of these retorts in discussions by Christians; I supplied these retorts on behalf of the Christians, and in supplementation of the investigation into their belief.

---

66. Cf. Samau'al, p. 24/42, and the medieval Jewish *Toledot Yeshu* tracts; also Matt. 12: 24.

## CHAPTER 4

# 67 *On the creed of the Muslims: concerning the prophethood of Muhammad, his miracles, the principles of his faith; on their opponents' inquiries in these matters; and a right course in reply to these inquiries.*

THE Muslims agree that Muḥammad Ibn 'Abdallāh Ibn 'Abd al-Muṭṭalib is the Messenger of God and Seal of the Prophets;[1] that he was sent to all mankind,[2] that he abrogated all the previous religions, and that his religion will remain in force to the day of resurrection; that he called upon men to believe in God and His angels, messengers, and scriptures, and to believe that God is one, has no companion, none like or similar to Him, no mate or child, and that God is preexistent, living, all-knowing, almighty, willing, hearing, seeing, speaking; and that He sent the Torah through Moses, the Gospel through Jesus, and sent prophets before and after Moses; that Muhammad, on behalf of God, announced that He commanded the performance of prayer, payment of Zakāt,[3] fasting during Ramaḍān,[4] pilgrimage to the sanctuary in Mecca; he enjoined also loyalty in contract, reverence toward parents, and other noble moral norms, and proscribed their opposites. They further agree that on public and private affairs Muhammad legislated numerous precepts contained in the Muslims' legal books; that he announced God would, on the day of resurrection, raise up the dead, call them to account for their beliefs

1. Koran 33: 40.
2. Koran 34: 27 (28).
3. Contribution to community chest for alms and social welfare in general.
4. Ninth month of the (lunar) Islamic calendar; period of fasting during daylight hours.

and deeds, and reward them according to merit. "Whoever has done a particle's weight of good shall see it and whoever has done a particle's weight of evil shall see it,"[5] and on that day all men will be divided into two factions, one in paradise, the other in the fire called hell.

Those who enter paradise will enjoy bliss eternal and unceasing, having whatever their souls may desire and whatever may please the eye, for in paradise there is of bliss what no eye has seen, no ear has heard, and what no human mind has thought of. There they will eat, drink, and marry.

According to most Muslims, if, despite having perpetrated a major sin, those who enter hell have recognized the 68
prophethood of Muhammad and his message, they will not
remain in fire eternally but will, after merited punishment or
through intercession and forgiveness, leave it for paradise.
Men who believe this admit that even forgiveness or intercession alone may save a soul from hell.

But there are Muslims who postulate that sinners eternally endure chastisement.

If those who enter Hell have not acknowledged the prophethood of Muhammad because his call was either not in their tongue or was understood in a manner discouraging speculation and quest—for example, if they heard that a deceiver called Muhammad had claimed prophethood and was followed by a great number of people who had been duped by his talk—they too will not remain in hell forever. If they did not believe, yet did not commit sins that would make them subject to chastisement, they will gain full mercy and never enter hell. If Muhammad's call reached them and stimulated their inquisitiveness, yet they denied his prophethood, though not out of obdurateness but because despite the utmost intellectual effort and speculation they did not grasp the veracity of that prophethood, then, in the view of some Muslim thinkers, such people would not be in hell forever or would not enter it at all, unless they deserved it for some other cause. Other Muslim authorities, however, have reached the conclusion that such

---

5. Koran 99: 7–8.

people would enter hell and sojourn in it forever, and they claim this is the consensus of Islamic opinion. But the truth of the claim of consensus in this matter is not ascertainable, and even if it is true, the authorities who have discussed the sources of law have decided that consensus is a proof only in hypothetical cases, not in actual ones.

Thus, in the view of the majority of Muslims, only those people who deny the prophethood of Muhammad out of stubbornness and out of deliberate neglect of quest will remain in hell forever and their chastisement will be more severe than that meted out to others. The few Muslims who hold a different view in this matter are dissenters of no importance.

Muslims differ about God's essence. Some are anthropomorphists, but others refrain from anthropomorphism.

They differ also about God's attributes, acts, and names, the circumstances of prophecies, reward and punishment, the true nature of faith and of Islam, and whether the angels are higher than the prophets or the prophets higher than the angels. They differ on matters of the *imamate* and on details of precepts. The extent of the dissension is almost impossible to record and is not relevant to our purpose.[6]

Muslims present six proofs for the veracity of Muhammad and his message.

69 **Proof One.**

He claimed being prophet and messenger, and the miracle appeared in accordance with his claim. Everyone of this description is prophet and messenger, so it follows that Muhammad is truly God's messenger.[7]

Now, if we say that such was his claim, it is because of transmitted tradition. If we say the miracle was wrought by him it is because the Koran which was revealed to him has

---

6. Such is the scope of manuals of Islamic theology, e.g., the treatises *al-Muḥaṣṣal* and *Ma'ālim* by Fakhr al-Dīn al-Rāzī frequently excerpted in this chapter.

Imamate: leadership in the Islamic community, office of the caliph. The problem is: Who is the rightful successor, especially as a faction (the Shī'a) insisted that the progeny of the Prophet were providential leaders.

7. Cf. *Ma'ālim*, p. 90.

been transmitted. The Koran is a miracle because Muhammad challenged the Arabs, who are supremely eloquent, to produce its equivalent, and they failed to do so. Anything of this nature is a miracle. His challenge regarding the Koran is indicated in verses such as:[8]

> "Say: verily if men and jinn agree to produce the like of this Koran, they will not produce the like of it though one to the other were backer";

or

> "Or do they say: 'he has invented it'; say [thou]: 'Then bring ten suras like it which have been invented";

or

> "Or do they say: 'He has invented it?' Say: 'Then produce a sura like it, and call upon whomsoever you are able [to call] apart from God";

or

> "if you are in doubt about what we have sent down to our servant, bring forward a sura like it, and call your witnesses apart from God, if you speak the truth."

It says further

> "If you do not do so—nor will you do it—"

Thus God, by some decisive judgment, denied Muhammad's adversary the ability to act.

Now these verses indicate that the challenge referred once to the Koran, once to ten suras thereof, and sometimes to one sura. It has the sound of a man in a contest for glory: produce a people like mine, like half of them, like one fourth of them, like one man of them.

The Arabs' failure to meet the challenge was mentioned because they had many motives for contesting, with no obstacle thereto, yet they offered no resistance; this indicates their failure therein. That they had motives is demonstrated by the fact that Muhammad forced Arabs to abandon their beliefs and leadership, imposed upon them duties that tired their bodies and diminished their wealth, and urged them to alienate their friends for reasons of religion; all these matters were hard on

8. Koran 17: 90; 11: 16; 10: 39 (38); 2: 21 (23); 2: 22.

them, especially as they were a most vehement people. If one man deprives another of his position of leadership, and calls upon that other to submit, then, no doubt, the latter party will attempt, with all possible means, to frustrate the former. As contesting certainly would have frustrated Muhammad's case, we conclude that the Arabs had numerous motives for contesting the Koran.

At the outset, the Arabs did not fear Muhammad, he feared them, which indicates the absence of any obstacle to their contesting him. That they did not contest Muhammad is indicated thus: had anybody come forward with a text to contest the Koran, such a text would have gained more fame than the Koran—because such a text would have cast doubt upon the Koran and would have served as a crushing argument against the proud pretender, and a thwart to his glory. There is no record of any contest so we must surmise that it did not occur. Clearly, if one has many reasons to perform a certain action and is unimpeded by obstacles, yet fails to pursue it, he is impotent. This is especially true for the Arabs, who chose an arduous struggle for life and death although contesting was easier. To swerve from the easier course to the arduous indicates the former is impossible. It is evident, therefore, that they found the easier task of contesting the Koran impossible to achieve.

Scholastics adduce and answer 15 queries on this matter.[9]

---

9. In Islamic theology the Koran is considered a miracle (*muʿjiz-a*), and the theory of the miraculous inimitability (*iʿjāz*) of the Koran is expounded in every manual of Islamic theology. But the sense of the miracle is in dispute: Is it that the language, style, form of the book are inimitable, or the exalted content? Or else, is it that the *inability* of the opponents of the Prophet *to contest when challenged* to do so constitutes the miracle? In this case the miracle consists of divine *deflection* (*ṣarf*) of the human ability from responding to the challenge. Cf. G. E. von Grunebaum, *Medieval Islam* (Chicago, 1946), pp. 96 ff.; *idem*, Introduction to *A Tenth-Century Document of Arab Literary Theory and Criticism* (Chicago, 1950); L. Gardet, *Dieu et la destinée de l'homme* (Paris, 1967), pp. 218 ff.; T. Andrae, *Die Person Muhammeds in Lehre und Glauben seiner Gemeinde* (Stockholm, 1917), pp. 94 ff.; Abdul Aleem in *Islamic Culture*, 1933.

### Query 1.

Is it impossible that another prophet, to whom the Koran had been revealed first, called Muhammad to his faith and to this book, and that he was then killed by Muhammad and, because the prophet's name was unknown, the book remained in Muhammad's hands?

### Reply.

Any fair and intelligent person who considers this query knows that this did not happen. Furthermore there are many passages in the Koran that show that the reference is to Muhammad, not to anybody else. This is clear to anyone reflecting on the circumstances related in the Koran regarding the Prophet's life, battles, family affairs, and conflicts with the hypocrites[10] and unbelievers.

### Query 2.

It is possible that Muhammad had read or heard the books of earlier prophets and had selected and compiled what was best in them; or that, attentive to the words of men, he studied them, chose and collected the more remarkable expressions and fine points and thus produced the Koran. Thus it is told on the authority of Abdallāh b. Sa'd b. Abī Sarḥ, the prophet's scribe:

> When the Prophet dictated to him the divine word
> Then we created the drop a clot
> Sa'd said:
> Blessed be God, the best of creators,
> And the Prophet said: write that down!
> So it was revealed.[11]

For this reason Abdallāh reverted to paganism. The story is frequently found in books on history and tradition. Such an

---

10. A term frequent in the Koran for a group of opponents in Medina.
11. On this scribe of the prophet cf. E.I.[2] I 51 f. The passage is Koran 23: 14. 'Abdallāh's exclamation was included in the Koran. To the pious it happened to coincide with an identical phrase in the revelation. 'Abdallāh used to take pride in having suggested improvement in the revealed verses, which led later to accusations that he had tampered with the text. He abandoned Islam but returned to the fold, and died as a Muslim chieftain some thirty-five years after the Prophet.

occurrence is not unfeasible, especially as the Koran was revealed to the Prophet over a prolonged period during which such slips could occur.

### Reply.

If this were true, the account of it would necessarily have
71 spread, as did the story of the aforementioned scribe. Again, either this compilation was supernatural, a miracle, or else it would have been contested.

### Query 3.

Even if we should admit that the text of the Koran has been transmitted, we do not concede that particulars of its verses have been [accurately] transmitted.

Thus the transmission of the verses concerning *the challenge* has not been established. It is reported that in the prophet's lifetime the Koran was memorized in its entirety by only six or seven persons. Therefore, collusion in distortion is not precluded. No one but the memorizers could have identified a changed and tampered-with passage.

It has been reported that Ibn Mas'ūd[12] denied that the first sura and the last two suras belonged to the Koran, but his companions held him in great esteem and none reproved him for his statement. Yet if anyone today were to deny that sura 108 is of the Koran,[13] he would be liable to anathema and death. It is, however, more evident that these suras belong to the Koran than that the verses concerning the *challenge* do.[14] Ibn Mas'ūd put "In the name of the merciful and compassionate God" at the head of the ninth sura; but neither Ubayy b. Ka'b[15] nor Zayd b. Ṯābit[16] did so. Ubayy included five suras in his copy which Ibn Mas'ūd excluded; Zayd excluded two

---

12. An early convert to Islam, he became an authority on the Prophet's teachings and on the Koran text. His text differed somewhat from the authorized version. Cf. *EI*² III 873 ff.

13. Consisting of three short verses, all in one line, it is the shortest chapter of the Koran.

14. Cf. n. 8, above.

15. An early believer, he served as secretary to the Prophet. Cf. Noeldeke, II, pp. 28, 30–39.

16. A young man from Medina, he became scribe to the Prophet, and

of them. They disagreed on whether "in the name of the merciful and compassionate God" is or is not a verse at the opening of the suras. Each declared the other's copy a forgery.

When, in the days of 'Uṯmān,[17] dissension among the people concerning the Koran increased he saw fit to burn all the versions except one. Ibn Mas'ūd said: If I reigned as they do, I should do to their copies what they did to mine. Ibn Mas'ūd would attack Zayd by saying: I read the Koran when he was still in the loins of his pagan father. It is reported that Ḥafṣa[18] possessed the volume of the Koran set by 'Umar. On the day Ḥfaṣa died, 'Uṯmān sent Marwān, then governor of Medina, to 'Abdallah b. 'Umar,[19] demanding that copy. Upon receiving
it. 'Uṯmān, fearing dissension, ordered that it be burned. 72
Verses would be sent to 'Umar[20] for verification, it is reported, and if he recognized them, he confirmed them; or he would accept them if the reporter was trustworthy, and in the event the reporter was not, 'Umar required the testimony of authorized witnesses from the reporter prior to acceptance. But this exposes the transmission of those verses to doubt.

There are dissensions regarding the words of the Koran, their order, and textual addition and deletion as well as the meaning. All this is known to the readers following the various "lections."[21] Yet it says in the Koran, "If it were from any other than God, they would find in it many disagreements."[22] Now, what disagreement is greater than this?

The verses on predestination, furthermore, contradict those on free will; verses directed against anthropomorphism contradict those that are anthropomorphic.

---

later served as high official under the early caliphs. He died in 45/665–666. Cf. *ibid.*, p. 54.

17. The third caliph (reigned 644–656).

18. Wife of the Prophet. Her father, 'Umar, became the second caliph. Cf. *EI*², III, pp. 63–65.

19. Son of the second caliph; brother of Ḥafṣa.

20. Second caliph (reigned 13–23/634–644).

21. A variety of readings is accepted as admissible and valid. They resulted from imperfections of the original notations and of the script itself (similarity of many letters; absence of short vowels).

22. Koran 4: 84 (82).

It is reported that when the [new] copy was completed and brought to 'Uṯmān he read it carefully, and said: "You have done well; it contains some irregularities but we shall correct that with our tongues."

The Koran is described as lucid and distinct which is incorrect because the letters that stand at the beginning of some suras are incomprehensible. Throughout the book, a dissenter can contest any verse with another verse or put on it a construction that will negate the original interpretation. The commentators who interpret the Koran find it extremely baffling and adduce various meanings for every verse.[23]

Although verses such as "We have not neglected anything in the book" and "nor a thing either full of sap or withered but is in a clear book" describe the Koran as containing all knowledge, we find it devoid of most problems, general and particular.[24]

The Koran contains much repetition and many platitudes such as "three days during the pilgrimage, and seven when ye return, that is ten altogether"[25]; and wrong order such as "Thee do we worship and on thee do we call for help"[26] though the appeal for help precedes the act. It says in the Koran "We never sent any messenger but with the speech of his people."[27] But the Quraysh, who are the prophet's people, do not use the *hamza*[28] while the Koran readers do. The division into chapters and verses is not definitely clear. These examples indicate the occasional distortion and deficient transmission [of the Koran].

**Reply.**

Should anybody attempt to alter the Koran at the present time by adding or subtracting words, it would be noticed; and

---

23. Cf. R. Bell, *Introduction to the Qur'an* (Edinburgh, 1953), pp. 54–57.

24. Koran 6: 38, 59.

25. Koran 2: 192.

26. Koran 1: 4. A wrong construction of the phrase was mentioned in discussions; cf. Noeldeke II, p. 36f.

27. Koran 14: 4.

28. (Sign of) the glottal stop.

we know that in the time of the Companions the public's opposition to a change in the Koran was perhaps stronger than 73
now. We must conclude, therefore, that the Koran has at no time been touched by distortion.

There was a group, though small in number, who had memorized every verse of the Koran, and their collective testimony served as proof [for the inclusion of a verse].

Ibn Mas'ūd's denial of suras 1, 113, 114, being parts of the Koran is a tradition of an individual and cannot be compared with transmission. And his denial, even if we accept it as correct, is simply a denial that the above chapters belonged to the Koran, rather than a denial that they were revealed to Muhammad. Perhaps, there are other criteria to be considered in divine revelation before it may be included in the Koran.

Even if the verses on the *challenge* were not intended to be included in the Koran, our argument holds as long as they are recognized as divine revelation. The same is true of the discussion of passages that are rejected by some but are included in Ibn Mas'ūd's copy.

The variations between copies and the final selection of one copy occurred because the Prophet, until his death, referred to the last copy to reach him, that of Zayd b. Ṯābit, in preference to the two previous copies, Ibn Mas'ūd's and Ubayy's. It is well known that he did not pray or recite with variant lections. The Muslims selected Zayd's copy because it was the latest presented to Muhammad. Thus it was God's choice for the prophet and the Muslims; Ibn Mas'ūd was the oldest of the three, and his version, consequently, had less of an audience than the other texts. It was more proper to accept Zayd's because he was the most recent of the three and his version the most widespread. The other versions, though true and sound, were barred lest dissension concerning the Koran should occur, thus causing it to become other than a [single] transmitted text.

The story of verses being brought to 'Umar is inadmissible because it stems from individual reports. The prophet himself was in charge of the collection of the Koran, as we can see from the agreement that the first Koran revelation in Mecca was "Recite in the name of thy Lord"[29] and in Medina, the sura *The Cow*,[30] and that the last was *Renunciation*.[31] Were it somebody else who collected it, not the prophet, he would have put the early material first, and the later further on. This shows they were following a text without innovating. This is true also of the agreement about the order of short and longer verses.

Dissent over the Koran is no argument against its divine origin. It does not follow from the verse "If it were from any other than God, they would find in it many a disagreement"
74 that if it were from God they would not find contradiction in it. To say "if this were black it would have color" does not presume that it is correct to say, "if this were not black it would have no color." We cannot admit that the Koran is invulnerable to all dissension, even if we disregard the above; the content of a verse may bring about dissension in some respects, but there is no dissension regarding variations in eloquence because generally even ordinary human speech, if extended, does not retain the same level of eloquence throughout.

As the prophet tells us, the various lections are all true and sound. The Koran was revealed in seven versions, each clear and sufficient.[32] By lections we mean variant words.

Scholars have, by the interpretations included in their works, eliminated the alleged contradiction between verses. They have said that the ambiguous revelations have their advantages in multiple reward, or that those people advocating a wrong opinion will persist in examining the text until they actually arrive at the truth.

When a book is described as lucid, that does not mean that it is entirely lucid. We do not concede that the Koran was described as containing all the sciences; this description more closely fits "the book," that is, the tablet preserved in heaven.

Philologists have mentioned several ways to eliminate the

---

29. Koran 96: 1.

30. Koran 2.

31. Koran 9. The early suras are at the end of the Koran.

32. Ibn Ḥanbal, V, p. 41. Cf. n. 21, above. *Mishkāt* 56.

charge of irregular usage in the Koran, as for example, the use of the wrong case.[33] If the report of ‘Uṯmān's phrase "there is some irregularity in it" is true, it must refer to an error in spelling.

The charge that the Koran contains wrong sequence, platitudes, and so on, has been discussed by the commentators.

Not only the Quraysh, but all the Arabs are the people of the prophet; the *hamza* occurs in the Koran because it appears in the language of Arabs other than the Quraysh.

Thus all the doubts rejected, it is established that both the particulars and the basic text of the Koran have been transmitted.

**I say:**

I found this to be the utmost the scholastics have to say on the subject.

But in my opinion this per se is insufficient to prove the point,* because the objector may say: Your assertion that the Companions' zeal to prevent any change in the Koran was as strong as the zeal of people today is the very point at issue. 75
The same holds true for your assertion that for every verse there was a group of memorizers and that transmission by them could serve as proof, or that the Prophet collected the Koran.

Numerous traditions in the two *Ṣaḥīḥs*[34] point in the opposite direction.

Thus Zayd b. Ṯābit said:

Abū Bakr sent for me at the time of the battle of the people of Yamāma.[35] ‘Umar was with him.

---

33. In Koran 20: 66 (63); Noeldeke, III, pp. n. 4; 5 n. 3; 70, 88.

* The Istanbul manuscript and the Tehran manuscript add: If it was not transmitted, transmission must be proved. Obviously this is not transmission proper. It would be more correct to argue that the transmission of the particulars of the Koran is self-evident and that discussion is superfluous. However, once argument is entered into, the opponent counters with argument.

34. The two major canonized collections of traditions (*ḥadīṯ*), edited by Bukhārī (d. 870) and Muslim (d. 875), respectively. Each of them is entitled *Ṣaḥīḥ*.

35. The campaign against the attempted secession (*ridda*) from the Islamic state and community in 633, following the death of Muhammad,

Abū Bakr related that 'Umar had come to him and said: The fighting was vehement in the battle of Yamāma and took a heavy toll of the reciters of the Koran, and I am afraid that the fighting may be vehement and take a heavy toll of the Koran reciters everywhere, and much of the Koran will be lost; I wish that you would order the collection of the Koran revelations.

Abū Bakr said:

How shall I do a thing that the Prophet has not done?

Said 'Umar:

By God, it is a good thing.

Abū Bakr:

'Umar kept on urging me until God filled me with the same conviction 'Umar held, and I came around to his view.

Zayd said that Abū Bakr had said:

You are a bright young man, impeccable; you used to write down the prophet's inspiration. So now trace the Koran and collect it.

Zayd said:

By God, had he charged me with transporting some mountain, it would not have been any harder for me than the collecting of the Koran. I said:

How do you do a thing the Messenger of God did not do?

Said Abū Bakr: By God, it is a good thing.

He kept urging me until God filled me with the same conviction and I came around to the view held by 'Umar and Abū Bakr. Then I traced the Koran fragments, collecting them from palm branches, patches, pieces of stone, and men's memory. I then found the end of sura 9: *There has come to you a messenger* (and so on to the end) with Kharīma b. Ṯābit or Abū Khuzayma, and I attached it to the proper sura. The sheets were with Abū Bakr during his lifetime until his death, then with 'Umar during

was conducted in Central Arabia and directed against the Banū Ḥanīfa tribe and its leader, the pretender to prophethood, Musaylima. The Muslim leader at the time was Abū Bakr, the first caliph (reigned 632–634).

his lifetime until his death, then with Ḥafṣa, 'Umar's daughter.

This is the end of the tradition.[36]

The "pieces of stone" are said to have been potsherds. There are many traditions to this effect, and some, when mentioning Abū Khuzayma, add:

I did not find it with anybody else.

This tradition contradicts the assertion that the prophet himself collected the Koran.

The various lections of the Koran, by numerous conflicting possible readings, such as *tabayyanū* and *taṯabbatū,** strongly indicate that the details of the Koran were not all transmitted or handed down by oral report but were sometimes taken unchecked from written texts, and this resulted in misreadings.

One faction of Muslims, considered evil by the other
Muslim groups, decided that distortion of the Koran did take 76
place, and that much of the Koran (originally twice its present size) had been eliminated because of the contest for the caliphate, and so on. They are among those who impugn the Companions. It is reported that sura 33 was the equal of sura 2.[37] Many scholars consider this possible and explained it by abrogation of passages. They also consider it possible that the devil, as well as hypocrites and their ilk, could falsify the Koran. It has been reported that when God revealed sura 53, the Prophet recited it until he reached the verse

Have ye considered Al-Lāt, and Al-'Uzzā, and the third, Manāt, the other [goddess]?[38]

the devil threw upon his tongue:

---

36. Bukhārī, III, p. 392. Cf. Noeldeke, II, pp. 11–15; R. Blachère, *Coran* (Paris, 1947), pp. 30–34.

* Cf. A. Jeffery, *Materials for the history of the text of the Qur'ān* (Leiden, 1937), p. 92: in the text of Koran 49:6 such differences were reported.

37. Sura 2 with its 286 verses is four times longer than sura 33 with its 73 verses. Cf. Noeldeke, I, p. 255.

38. Koran 53: 19–20.

> These are the swans exalted; whose intercession is to be hoped for.

When the Quraysh heard that, they rejoiced and said: he mentioned our deities most favorably. But as evening fell, Gabriel came to the prophet and said: Thou hast recited unto the men what I did not bring thee. Then the Prophet was seized with fear and sadness, so God revealed:

> We have not sent before thee any messenger or prophet but that when he formed his desire Satan threw [something] into his formulation.[39]

And the Prophet was yearning to receive a revelation with which he could approach his people.[40]

The opponents may also say:

We, by ourselves, would find the particulars of the Koran to be true provided they were transmitted in the same manner as its basic text, the existence of Muhammad, and his claim to prophethood, which are things we feel to be true. But though we have tried, we are less certain about the Koran than we are about the rest. If we felt the decision forming in our minds it would not be necessary for us to refute those quotations with counter-quotations. Further, how can alleged transmission be proved by such words? Useless against slight suspicion, how can they induce certainty of truth? Thus it is clear that once we presume that confirmation of the transmission of the particulars must be established, something more positive than the well-known assertion in the scholastic books is needed.

**Query 4.**

We do not concede that the *challenge* verses, supposing that we accept their transmission, truly prove the *challenge*; their purpose, rather, is to put forward claims in the customary
77 style of the speeches and poems of orators and poets. If their purpose had been to prove Muhammad's prophethood, this point, like the claim to prophethood itself, would have become well known outside the Koran. But not one chronicler reports that the prophet used the Koran against his opponents to

39. Koran 22: 51 (52).
40. Noeldeke, I, pp. 100–103.

argue the truth of his prophethood; nor is any of the prophet's believers reported to have become a believer because of the Koran. It is clear then that Muhammad did not rely upon the Koran to establish his own prophethood.

**Reply.**

It is possible that the Koran made the matter so well known that it obviated the urge to report the challenge elsewhere because it makes little sense to multiply channels.

**I say:**

This is a weak point, and its weakness is no secret to him who knows the historical works, the reports about the prophet, and the way he urged Islam upon people who came to him without any knowledge of the Koran, let alone the *challenge* verses; and who knows also how Muhammad's believers, during and after his time, urged Islam upon nonbelievers. When the Prophet wrote epistles to the Persian king, the Byzantine emperor, and other kings, he did not include the argument of the *challenge* to imitate the Koran. His Companions urged Islam upon those who had heard nothing of Muhammad, let alone of the Koran in general or particular passages of the Koran. There is no report that any *Companion* mentioned the *challenge* of the miracle of the Koran, or stressed that the Arabs had failed to produce anything resembling it (although they had ample reasons for doing so with nothing to prevent them, and so on) so that this might serve as a proof to other nations before they were fought and slain. This is the more notable because most of those nations spoke no Arabic, and learned nothing of the miracle of the Koran merely by listening to it—just as we, our knowledge of Arabic notwithstanding, are not aware of this miracle except through the use of this argument.

When the Muslims, fearing the Meccans, migrated from Mecca to Ethiopia, and the Negus, king of Ethiopia, asked them about their faith, the reported reply did not go beyond this:

> O, King, we were an ignorant people worshiping idols, eating carcass, doing loathsome things, ignoring kinship, forgetful of neighborliness, the strong among us devour- 78

> ing the weak; thus we lived until God sent us a messenger from our midst, known to us by his origin, truthfulness, reliability and chastity, and he called upon us to turn to God, to believe in one God, worship Him, reject for His sake our ancestors' belief in stone and idol, and commanded us to do such and such, and so on.[41]

But nothing was said of arguments about a miracle, Koranic or otherwise, although one would expect that in such accounts the *miracle* argument would come up, and that the reasons for mentioning the transmission and the particulars of the *challenge* would not vary with any group or any individual. Similarly, although prophetism, monotheism, and so on, are mentioned in the Koran, they also appear in such accounts, so every sensible person will conclude that had the *challenge* proved prophethood, it would have become well known.

Indeed, two Muslim scholars of the Mu'tazila school, Hishām al Fūṭī and 'Abbād al-Ṣaymarī, denied that the Prophet challenged people by claiming the inimitability of the Koran.[42] I found this evidence in the book *al-Shāmil fī Uṣūl al-Dīn* by al-Juwaynī, Imām al-Ḥaramayn,[43] who repudiated the two scholars. Undoubtedly, a great many people embraced Islam because upon hearing the Koran they were impressed by its stories of prophets, admonitions, parables, inducement and terror, assurance and warning, nay by its eloquence and peculiarity of style. As somebody said, it has sweetness and grace about it, and it is truly a discourse excellent and unexcelled. But it does not make an issue of the *challenge* as do the prophets about their miracles.

**Query 5.**

The report of the *challenge*, no doubt, did not reach the entire world, and perhaps some eloquent Arab happened to be on a trip to some distant land not reached by the report about Muhammad; had that Arab heard the *challenge* he would have been able to take up the contest.

---

41. Ibn Isḥāq, pp. 219 f.

42. Ninth-century theologians, teacher and disciple (cf. *EI*²).

43. Jurist-theologian (419–478/1028–1085), teacher of Ghazālī. *EI*² II 605.

**Reply.**

If the difference between the Koran and the speech of the eloquent men whom the report of the *challenge* did reach amounted to inimitability, then this argument is false. If it did not amount to that, the eloquent men present should have 79
said: The difference between the speech of the Koran and our speech does not amount to inimitability; and then the Koran would not serve as proof of prophethood.

**Query 6.**

Why is it impossible that the eloquent among the Arabs seeking leadership and kingship—and knowing they were possible only by a trick—secretly appointed Muhammad to leadership, and, by feigning enmity toward him and failure to contest the Koran as a miracle, thus made the Koran proof of his prophethood in the eyes of other people. This would have enabled the eloquent Arabs to attain their goal.

**Reply.**

We know definitely that among his enemies were the most distinguished of the eloquent, and their fates were various. Some of them died as unbelievers, for example, al-A'shā;[44] others embraced Islam after expressing such extreme enmity that the Prophet declared it was lawful to slay them, for example, Ka'b b. Zuhayr;[45] others, again, after embracing Islam, did not succeed in achieving the necessary acceptance, for example, Labīd b. Rabī'a[46] and Nābigha al-Ja'dī.[47] If it had been as suggested, the prophet, upon attaining power, would have granted those eloquent persons their due for their effort, which, necessarily, would have been apparent to his enemies, who would have publicized it, and thus thwarted his claim. If treachery, would have swerved from support to opposition, he had refused them their due, they, after discussing his either, if they feared him, after emigration to another land, or

44. *LHA*, p. 124.

45. R. A. Nicholson, *Eastern Poetry and Prose* (Cambridge, 1922), pp. 19–23.

46. *LHA*, pp. 119–121.

47. Died 65/684 (*GAL*, Suppl. I, p. 93).

at the seat of his rule if they did not. Also, if that collusion of all the eloquent had taken place, it would have proved impossible to keep it concealed from the enemies exclusively. If the collusion was not comprehensive, those who were no party to it had many reasons to contest the Prophet, and would have done so.

**Query 7.**

Assuming that Muhammad's foes had enough reasons to thwart his cause, why should those reasons take that particular form, that is, of the contest of the *challenge*?

80 **Reply.**

If there are several roads to reach a goal, of course the easiest and most direct will be chosen. It is, therefore, an obvious conclusion of all sensible persons that the easiest way to contest Muhammad was to produce something equal to the Koran, if possible—in the same manner that boys rush to compete against a boy who claims superiority in jumping over a river or in hitting a target.

**Query 8.**

We do not concede that contesting is preferable to other methods, for this is not self-evident. The Arabs may have believed that warfare was essentially more effective or they may have swerved from it fearing that dissent might occur as to whether it was or was not an act of contesting. Or perhaps producing something like the Koran, as suggested by the prophet, posed problems for them: in doubt as to whether their efforts should deal with eloquence or poetic form, or both, or with disclosure of the hidden, or with subtle points, they decided to switch to another method of contesting. Or perhaps Muhammad's initial weakness and fear of them caused them to ignore contesting him, until he had gained overwhelming power and pursued the path of power, not the path of argumentation. When he was able to wage war upon them, he did so, thus leaving them with no occasion to contest him. Further, it is evident to all who study the history books and reports that there is no mention in the Koran of his challenging them. It is also possible that the eloquent did not feel impelled to contest him because it was apparent to them that their orations and poems were more eloquent than his Koran.

**Reply.**

The ultimate purpose in war is to slay the rival, but this does not necessarily mean defeat of an argument. Further, people are not sure of victory in war, and are in danger. Not so in contest. How can it be said, then, that war is a better choice than the contest? Had he started with contest, before war, his army might have scattered altogether, or a great part of it, for it is impossible to keep a mass of people in a state of pertinacity. Contest, then, would have proved easier. But as the opponents waged war repeatedly without success, it follows that they were forced to give up *contesting*.

The Arabs did not consider the prophet disreputable even at the first, before hijra, and this is evident because they were intent on denouncing him, fulminating against him, cursing him, and on finding ways to thwart his cause, all of which is clearly not done in the case of an inconsequential person.

Dispute over whether or not their action constituted contesting is merely a matter of degree: If they produced something approximating the Prophet's speech, then the Prophet's speech would no longer be inimitable. Furthermore, the belief of some that contesting did occur is preferable to the total belief that they failed therein. If they were in doubt as to the 81
nature of the imitation, they could, what with the length of time, inquire about it. Indeed, although the *challenge* was unspecified in nature, their silence regarding specification indicates that they were well aware of what the *challenge* consisted.

The rise of the Prophet's power did not mean that the urge to oppose him necessarily had to slacken; it is possible that because he insisted on power, he would accept no argument, and when he failed to engage in argument his cause might have become confused and some of his supporters might have defected.

Nobody, furthermore, has concluded that their orations and poems are more eloquent than the Koran. The point in contention is this: Is it true or not that the disparity between Muhammad's speech and theirs amounted to a miracle? If it is, a sensible man must solve the doubt that may have found its way into his mind: Why, then, did not the people demonstrate the superiority of their speech over his?

**Query 9.**

He may have diverted them from the contest by warfare, forcing them to refrain from the contest in fear of his associates. This could be analogous to a people failing to rebuff a vicious book authored by their king.

**Reply.**

This is an extremely weak point, because war did not prevent them from writing lampooning poems. The war, furthermore, was not permanent, and was not fought by all the Arabs, nor was it fought before the time of the hijra. If it had been war that diverted them, they would have said: Abandon warfare, and give us time to contest you.

**Query 10.**

How do you know that the Koran was not contested? It is possible that it was contested but word of it did not spread and the report thereof did not come down to us. Many significant matters are not widely known, for example, whether or not suras 1, 113, and 114 are of the Koran, and whether the second call to prayer is single or double. Or take the "clear title" to the caliphate as claimed by the Shi'a.[48] If it is true, it was not widely known; if it is false, it is the report on how it was concocted that did not spread; in either case, a major event [was not reported].

**Reply.**

82 There can be no comparison between the eagerness of the dissenters in these questions and the eagerness of the enemies of Islam to impugn Muhammad's prophethood. Yet the dissension on the questions mentioned *was* reported generally, even though no agreement has been reached about it. But the

---

48. The Shī'a, contending that the succession to the Prophet was to be reserved to 'Alī (son-in-law of the Prophet, husband of the Prophet's daughter, Fāṭima) and his progeny, claimed that the Prophet had designated 'Alī as imām, head of the community. The Shī'a circulated texts in support of this claim. On the discussion whether in the second call to prayer the formulas are to be uttered once only or repeatedly, cf. *EI*[2] *s.v.* Iḳāma.

contesting was not reported *at all*. It is clear, then, that it did not take place.

**Query 11.**

We may admit that reports of great affairs must spread, but we may admit it only on condition that they not be prevented. It is possible that there was one contestant or even two contestants; that the contest was first offered to Muhammad or one of his companions; and that the contestant was slain to conceal the matter—or perhaps the bid was concealed by the opponents for reasons of fear or other factors.

**Reply.**

The reply to the above is clear from earlier replies.

**Query 12.**

It is said that the prophet was contested by the Arabs' seven odes,[49] by Musaylima's words,[50] by al-Naḍr b. al-Ḥāriṯ's stories of the Persian kings,[51] and that he was also contested after his time by Ibn al-Muqaffaʻ,[52] Qābūs b. Washmigīr,[53] and al-Maʻarri.[54]

**Reply.**

It is obvious that poetry and stories do not come under the category of contest, for the *challenge* was one of eloquence and style combined, not of eloquence alone. The words of Musaylima and the others do not approximate the Koran, nor is it a condition of proving the miracle true that there should be found nothing like it at some future time.

**Query 13.**

Perhaps Muhammad was more eloquent than others, and that is why they were unable to contest him. There may be an

49. A collection of pre-Islamic poems (*Muʻallaqāt*). Cf. A. J. Arberry, *The Seven Odes* (London, 1957).

50. Claimed prophethood in Central Arabia, in the last years of Muhammad (cf. n. 35, above).

51. "I can tell a better story than he [Muhammad]," said Naḍr, introducing his tale (Ibn Isḥāq, pp. 191, 235).

52. Official, translator, author, of Persian origin; one of the creators of Arabic literary prose; executed *ca.* 760.

53. Persian prince (976–1012).

54. Poet (973–1057). *LHA*, pp. 313–324; R. A. Nicholson, *Studies in Islamic Poetry* (Cambridge, 1921).

expert in a craft, unequalled by his contemporaries and perhaps by craftsmen over hundreds of years. For instance, there are masters of learning, such as Aristotle in logic, Euclid in
83 geometry, Ptolemy in astronomy, as well as magicians whom none could contest in their time. Ibn Zakaryā[55] narrates that he saw a man who uttered clearly whatever he wanted through his armpit, and there was nobody to contest with him. But this is no indication of that man's prophethood.

**Reply.**

In all these cases the difference between the respective parties does not amount to the miraculous, which it does in the case of the Koran versus other speech.

**I say:**

It is not evident, nor do we find a proof, that the difference between the eloquence of the Koran and other eloquent speech amounts to the miraculous. If it were so, nobody would differ about it; yet a large number of Muslim scholars, such as most of the Mu'tazila,[56] some of the orthodox, and others, did not accept it, and taught that Koranic eloquence is similar to other speech, and that its miraculous character consists, rather, of the *deflection*—that is, of God depriving the opponents of their ability to produce anything resembling it, though they should have been able to do so. It was as if one said: my miracle is that these healthy individuals cannot move their hands. If they cannot, his miracle has come true.

This opinion that the miracle consists of *deflection* has been disproved for three reasons.

First, if the Arabs had known of the *deflection*, they would have talked about this miracle with wonder, and the

---

55. al-Rāzī (Rhazes of medieval Latin writings), physician-philosopher (d. 925). Cf. A. J. Arberry, *The Spiritual Physick of Rhazes* (London, 1950).

56. School of rationalizers in Islamic theology. Availing themselves of Hellenic and Hellenistic material they tried to represent Islam in rational terms purging it of seeming contradictions and difficulties in its canonized scripture and traditions. Flourished in the eighth to tenth centuries. They fought Manichaean influences strong among the educated at the time.

report of it would have spread and been transmitted because it is natural to discuss extraordinary things. And nothing prevented the opponents from discussing it because they would have simply ascribed it to witchcraft, so their confession of failure would not have been an admission that Muhammad's argument against them was valid. Thus it must have been discussed.

Second, if the miracle consisted of the *deflection,* then the
poorer the Koran the greater the miracle. It is as if one said: My 84
true proof is that I can lift a mana,[57] and nobody but I can do so. This would constitute a miracle, but would not if he had said, "I can transport a thousand mana." The latter merely implies his greater strength, but that is not a proof of prophethood. Thus, the theory of *deflection* is impossible unless the Koran is not very eloquent. But it is of the utmost eloquence, and it is, therefore, no miracle unless it is as extraordinary as the claimant who can lift 10,000 or 100,000 mana measures.

The third is that if *deflection* was true, his opponents would have opposed the prophet with their speech before he had challenged them with the Koran. If it is said that their speech had not been previously of that prophetic genre, we say: the miracle, then, is eloquence plus that genre, not *deflection.* And if *deflection* is dismissed and the Koran is not purported to reach the state of the miraculous in eloquence or some other respect, then the opponent's doubt of the Koran as a miracle prevails. The scholastics' discussion on this point is then unsatisfactory.

Further, what was said, even if it be correct, is no fit answer to the doubt about the man who spoke through his armpit, because he might claim that therein he had reached the range of the miraculous.

**Query 14.**

The prophet endured hardships during the long period of time that he gathered the Koran together. Nobody else displayed such endurance, and of course nobody else produced

57. A measure of weight.

anything resembling the Koran. As Ibn Zakaryā[58] says: there was a man who did not eat, for 27 days, to my knowledge, because he had developed that habit, and yet he was strong of body.

**The Reply**

is identical with the one already given. In addition, the difference between random speech and oratory is slight in a person of perfect eloquence; but we find the prophet's normal
85 speech[59] seemed to be as different from the language of the Koran as the speech of any other man. Further, he had challenged them about the Koran in Mecca for 13 years, and since he did not fight them there, they should have had time enough to contest him then.

**I say:**

You know what I have said about the replies to previous queries. What has been added here is very weak, and the reader cannot fail to notice it.

**Query 15.**

The Arabs had no knowledge about God and His attributes, creation, angels, prophets, paradise, and hell; Muhammad had knowledge of all these matters. He urged them to contest him by presenting these or similar matters with eloquence and rhythm. But since they were ignorant of these matters, they recognized the greatness of the Koran, and failed to produce anything to equal it.

**Reply.**

There were Jews and Christians present. The Arabs must have learned these matters from them and must have expressed them eloquently. There were even eloquent Jews and Christians among the Arabs who should have taken charge of this contest.

**One could**

pose many queries in discussing the Koran. I will mention those the scholastics do not mention. All these and similar

---

58. Cf. note 55, above.

59. That is, everyday speech, apart from the Koran.

queries have been answered in a general reply cited by the *imām* Fakhr al-Dīn al-Rāzī[60] in the *Kitāb-al-Ma'ālim.*

This is the way it is: Even if we grant that the Koran does not attain the range of the miraculous in perfection, we know it is indubitably a noble, exalted, precious, wise, and eloquent book. Muhammad, furthermore, grew up in Mecca, a city void of books of scholarship and research. Muhammad travelled only twice briefly, and he did not apply himself to reading and learning. Forty years of his life passed in this way. Then,
after he turned forty, there appeared unto him this book. This 86
is a great miracle because it is impossible that a book of this nature would, without divine guidance, revelation, and inspiration, appear to a man lacking all research, study, reading, and erudition. This is self-evident, and it is the meaning of the verse

> If ye are in doubt about what we have sent down to our servant, bring forward a sura like him,[61]

that is, like Muhammad, without reading, study, or learning from scholars. Here, then, is a strong point and a clear proof.

This is the substance of what I found in *Kitāb al-Ma-'ālim.*[62] It is better than the detailed replies, but it needs the support of intuition when other concomitants join it. While the given interpretation of the verse quoted is not generally accepted, it is irrelevant to the argument which is complete without it.

**Proof Two**

is that Muhammad announced mysteries. This is a miracle which proves he was right in claiming prophethood and apostolate as has been asserted, and he consequently is truly the messenger of God. Let us discuss the mysteries announced by him. They are of two kinds: one refers to times prior to Muhammad and the other to times after him. The former are utterances about events affecting earlier people, which he

---

60. Famous theologian (543–606/1149–1209).

61. Koran 2: 21 (23). The text is usually taken to end: like *it.*

62. *Ma'ālim,* p. 90 ff.

made without the benefit of reading a book or drawing upon any man; as for the latter, some occur in the Koran and some in traditions. The best known in the Koran are ten in number.[63]

The first is the passage:

*All of them will be routed and will turn their backs*[64] and this came true on the day of the battle of Badr.

The second is:

. . . *When God promised you that one of the two parties should be yours,*[65] and theirs it was.

The third is:

*Say to the nomads left behind: you will be summoned against a people of warlike spirit,*[66] as indeed they were, both in battling the Banū Ḥanīfa and in the war against Persia.

The fourth is:

*A.L.M. The Romans have been defeated in the nearer part of the land. But after their defeat they will be victorious in a few years*[67] and that is what happened.

The fifth is:

*We shall show them our signs in the skies and in themselves,*[68] which alluded to the people of Mecca; and it happened as he had said it would.

The sixth is:

*He who imposed the Koran upon thee shall certainly restore thee to a place of return,*[69] that is, to Mecca; and he was restored to it.

The seventh is:

*That He may make it pre-eminent above all religions,*[70] and He did make it [Islam] pre-eminent.

87 The eighth is:

63. The list occurs in *Arbaʿīn*, pp. 313 f. and 315 f.

64. Koran 54: 45.

65. Koran 8: 7. The reference is to a caravan seized by the Muslims.

66. Koran 48: 16. Cf. n. 34, above.

67. Koran 30: 1–3. The unexplained letters are included in the text.

68. Koran 41: 53.

69. Koran 28: 85.

70. Koran 9: 33; 48: 28; 61: 9.

*God has promised to those of you who believe and have wrought the works of righteousness, that He will surely make you successors [to power] in the land*[71] and He made a number of the Prophet's companions successors.

The ninth is:

*. . . desire death if ye speak the truth. But they will never desire it,*[72] in an allusion to the Jews and what they desired.

The tenth is:

*Humiliation and poverty were stamped upon them.*[73] [The truth of] this became clear from the fact that after this word no forceful power appeared among the Jews.

There are also ten non-Koranic instances that are best known, and all of them were fulfilled.[74]

The first is:

*The earth contracted for me and I was shown its east and west, and the realm of my community will reach what was contracted of it for me.*[75]

The second is:

The Prophet's word to 'Adī b. Ḥātim: *What would you say [about a time] when a woman could leave the farthest point of Yemen for the farthest point of al-Ḥīra, fearing none but God.*[76]

The third is:

That he announced the death of the Negus, and later the reports of his death spread.[77]

The fourth is:

The prophet's word to 'Ammār b. Yāsir: *the iniquitous faction will kill you.*[78]

The fifth is:

The Prophet's word to Ali: *the most villainous of men is he who hocks the she-camel and he who dyes this one with this*

71. Koran 24: 54 (55).
72. Koran 62: 6–7.
73. Koran 2: 58 (61).
74. Cf. n. 63, above.
75. Ibn Ḥanbal, V, p. 278.
76. *Ibid.*, IV, p. 257; Ibn Isḥāq, pp. 947 ff. Bukhārī II 202 f. Miskhāt 1259.
77. Bukhārī, "Janā'iz" 4, I, p. 315; "Manāqib al-Anṣār" 38, III, p. 28 f.
78. Ibn Ḥanbal, II, p. 161.

*one, that is, dyes your beard with the blood of your head.*[79]

The sixth is:

The Prophet's word to Ali: *You will be fighting the oath violators and the iniquitous and the defectors.*[80]

The seventh is:

The Prophet's word: *Follow the two who [will be] after me, Abū Bakr and 'Umar.*[81] Thus he announced that they would survive him.

The eighth is:

His word: *The caliphate after me is for 30 years,*[82] which is the period of the caliphate of the righteous caliphs.

The ninth is:

That on the night of ascension he announced to Quraysh certain matters; then the Quraysh inquired about them, and it was as he had said.[83]

The tenth is:

That he said to al-'Abbās at the time of the latter's capture: *Ransom yourself and your nephews for you are wealthy. 'Abbās said: I have no money. Said the Prophet: where is the money which you deposited in Mecca with Umm al- Faḍl*
88 *when nobody was with you two, and about which you said: 'If I am hurt on my trip, so much to al-Faḍl and to 'Abdallah so much.' Then 'Abbas said: By Him who has sent you, truly, nobody but I have known this.' He embraced Islam, and so did 'Aqīl.*[84]

**Discussion of mysteries.**

It has been stated in discussing the annunciation of mysteries that we do not concede the transmission of the verses containing them. This doubt was contained in the state-

---

79. *Ibid.*, IV. pp. 263 (cf. Koran 91: 12–14).

80. Quoted in Qāḍī Nu'mān, *Da'ā'im al-Islām,* ed. A. Fayzi (Cairo, 1963), I, p. 388 (indicated by Prof. J. Eliash); 'Abd al Jabbār, *Sharḥ al-uṣūl al Khamsa* (Cairo, 1965), p. 637.

81. Ibn Ḥanbal, V, p. 382; Ibn Sa'd, II:2, pp. 98 line 20 f.

82. Ibn Ḥanbal, V, p. 221.

83. Referring to the Prophet's night journey to a distant sanctuary, identified as that of Jerusalem (Bukhārī, III, p. 30; Ibn Isḥāq, pp. 265, 267). *Miskhāt* 1270.

84. Ibn Ḥanbal, I, p. 353; Ibn Sa'd, Iv:1, pp. 8 ff. Cf. *Muḥaṣṣal,* p. 152.

ment concerning the verses of challenge. We do not concede the veracity of the traditions in the matter because they are individual reports. Even if we should concede the truth thereof, we do not admit that announcing mysteries is miraculous. Astrologers, magicians, and dream interpreters may announce similar things.

Through reliable transmission we know that there was in Baghdad a blind woman who announced hidden things in detail. Abū-l-Barakāt,[85] author of *Kitāb al-Mu'tabar,* said that he had tested her until he became certain that she was announcing hidden things without any fraud or falsification. It says in Ibn al-Jauzī's *History*[86] that though Baghdad's bright minds tried their best they could not discover any trick. The woman appeared in the year 501 of the hijra (= 1107–8).

Sometimes people given to devotional exercises and mysticism reach a stage when they are able to announce mysteries. There are numerous similar reports about the Barāhima. Muslims agree that Saṭīḥ, Suwayd b. Qārib, Qusā and others of the (pagan) Arab soothsayers could announce mysteries, and that they had announced the advent of Muhammad.[87]

Furthermore, announcing mysteries will be a miracle only if it is exceptional rather than habitual.

What the Prophet, peace upon him, announced, is not exceptional because some of it is vague, such as *Ye shall certainly enter the sacred mosque,*[88] and includes no explanation regarding the time, the number of people to enter, or the nature of the entrance (peaceful or forceful). An announcement of this sort will rarely prove wrong because its truth is

---

85. Distinguished philosopher in Baghdad in the twelfth century. In old age he converted from Judaism to Islam (cf. S. Pines in *EI*², I, pp. 111 ff.; *idem,* "From Abū-l-Barakāt's Commentary on Ecclesiastes," *Tarbiz,* v. 33 (1963), pp. 198–213.

The passage referred to is in the *Kitāb al-Mu'tabar,* ed. S. Yaltkaya (Hyderabad, 1358/1939), II, pp. 433 f.

86. This author died in 501/1107–1108, and the reference is to *Al-Muntaẓam* (Hyderabad, 1359/1940), IX, pp. 157 f.

87. Cf. *EI* or *SEI,* s.v. Kāhin; T. Fahd, *La divination arabe* (Leiden, 1966), s.v.

88. Koran 48: 27.

easily established if anyone enters. Further, if the time is not specified, and a semblance of what the announcer had promised occurs, he turns it into proof that he was right; if it does not occur, he says: I have not specified the time of its occurrence, and it will occur later. We find many artful astrologers and others doing this, and simple folk imagine them to be right.

Some of the Prophet's utterances are platitudes, for example, *but they will never desire it.*[89] It is evident that most
89 people will not desire to die.

Some of Muhammad's words are those of optimism and are intended to strengthen the hearts of followers, as is customary with leaders who encourage partisans in fighting their foes. The leaders promise them that they, the partisans, will prevail and will sway power. Of this type is the verse *God has promised to those of you who have believed and wrought the works of righteousness, that He will surely make them successors [to power] in the land;*[90] also *A.L.M. The Romans have been defeated in the nearer part of the land.*[91]

These three categories of the Prophet's words are not in conflict with the ordinary, and consequently are not miraculous.

Also, in regard to events of the past, it is not impossible that the Prophet heard them from others and remembered them. Indeed, he was suspected of this. The Koran reproduces the word of the unbelievers: *These are nothing but tales of the ancients which he has written for himself! They are recited to him morning and evening.*[92] Also *when Our signs are recited to him he says: "Tales of the ancients."*[93] Considering that he traveled twice to Syria, a land of Jews and Christians, before he was called upon to be a prophet, it cannot be thought unlikely that he heard these tales from another person.

Moreover, there was a group of Jews and Christians

---

89. Koran 25:6.
90. Koran 24: 54 (55).
91. Koran 30: 1.
92. Koran 25: 6 (5); cf. 23: 85, 27: 70.
93. Koran 68:15.

among the Arabs, and it is not unlikely that he had heard stories from them. Were it not so, why did he not tell stories relating to things after his time with the same degree of detail that marks his tales about what had happened before his time?

The foretelling of the future was not proved until the events occurred. But the faith of those who recognized his prophethood did not depend on the occurrence of these announcements, such as *entering the sacred mosque* or *the Romans have been defeated.* The proof of prophethood is not contained in these announcements, and they are not needed in order to establish his prophethood.

**Reply.**

"In establishing the prophethood of Muhammad, peace upon him, we do not rely on this aspect only. To establish his apostolate, we rely, rather, upon the revelation of the Koran to him. Other aspects such as the aforementioned are mentioned as complements, not as an independent proof." Thus answered the imām Fakhr al-Dīn al-Rāzī in the *Kitāb al-Muḥaṣṣal,*[94] although in the book *Nihāyat al-ʿUqūl* he left a detailed reply which I have not mentioned here because of its
weakness, a weakness of which he undoubtedly was aware. 90

**I say:**

In the books of the Muslim theologians it is asserted that the Jews and Christians do not object at all to the Prophet's stories of antiquity. But we find that Jews and Christians do contest many of them, such as the story of Solomon, the son of David, and how he subdued the wind and the *jinn*; how he knew the language of the birds, conversed with the hoopoe, and sent it to the queen of Sheba, whose throne was brought to him; about his death, how the beast of the earth gnawed his staff, and the people learned that the *jinn* had not known of Solomon's death until he collapsed or else they would not have persevered in their humiliating punishment.[95]

---

94. *Muḥaṣṣal,* p. 155, lines 23–24.

95. Cf. *SEI,* s.v. Sulayman. In the Koran, Sulayman (Solomon) dies while sitting on his throne. The jinn, unaware of his death, continue for a year to build the temple. The beast (traditionally the white ant) gnawed the royal staff, and when it collapsed, the king's body fell down. That

The same is true of the story of Jesus: that the Jews had not crucified him but had been made to think they had; that his mother was the daughter of 'Imrān and the sister of Aaron.[96]

The same is true of the story of 'Uzayr, that the Jews declared him the son of God; also of their statement that God's hand is fettered [literally or in the sense that God is avaricious].[97]

All this is the opposite of what is transmitted by Jews and Christians.

The most repugnant story to them is that of Solomon, for the Jews carry a detailed tradition of his food, wealth, number of wives, stables of horses, years of kingship, length of his life, many of the parables and proverbs that he uttered, his constructive activity in the land, etc. But they doubt not that this particular story is without foundation. Were there any truth in it, it would be more proper for the Jews to carry the tradition than to leave it to somebody else's version. After all, the Jews wish to glorify Solomon, who was one of their kings and of their faith.

Neither the Jews nor the Christians doubt that Jesus, the son of Mary, was crucified, and they transmit the story of his crucifixion with the same certainty as that of his existence. The name of the father of Maryam, the mother of Jesus was, according to the Christians, Joakhin.[98] Maryam had no brother.

There is no tradition by the authority of any Jew that 'Uzayr was the son of God, or that God's hand is fettered, either in the literal sense or in reference to avarice. If any of them said that, he would be considered among them an unbeliever and outside their community.

---

proved that the jinn's knowledge was defective (Koran 27: 16–44; 34: 13; 38: 36).

96. Cf. *SEI,* s.v. Isa. Koran 4: 156–157 (it only seemed to the Jews that they crucified Jesus); concerning the mother of Jesus, Koran 3: 31 and 19: 29.

97. Koran 9: 30 and 5: 69 (64). On Ezra-'Uzayr, cf. *SEI.*

98. A traditional name, not occurring in canonic scriptures.

The stories mentioned in the Koran and in tradition that are contested by Jews and Christians are too numerous for close examination.

Perhaps the scholastics were alluding to the fact that 91
among the Prophet's contemporaries those Jews and Christians of Arab descent were the ones who were not contesting the Koran stories; they did not contest these stories either because the Koran stories had not all reached them, or because these Jews and Christians were ignorant, even as many of the nomadic Arabs are in our time. Perhaps, also, they were afraid to declare their denial and refutation, and kept silent.

The basis of this complete rejection is the denial of the soundness of transmission, which point has been discussed previously.

**Proof Three.**

The Muslim traditions include accounts of many miracles by Muhammad, for example, water welling up between his fingers, feeding many people with little food, the split of the moon, the yearning of the wood, the complaint of the she-camel before him, and so on, all of which are contained in the books of *traditions*.[99] Though all of these cannot claim full transmission, still transmission points to the veracity of some. Whichever it may be, the object of having a miraculous deed on record is achieved. Of course, this will happen only to a prophet, or it will be contested. But it is known that these were not contested. Hence, they point to the prophethood of Muhammad.

**Against This.**

It might be said that if these things had happened, they would have been carried by an uninterrupted tradition, as they are wondrous things and there are many motives for carrying a tradition of wondrous things. But as the matters in question have not been carried by an uninter-

---

99. Cf. *Muḥaṣṣal*, pp. 151 f. Water welling up: Bukhārī, I, p. 55; II, p. 396; III, 111. Feeding: II pp. 109 f., 142, 243 f.; III, pp. 94, 493 f. Splitting the moon, *ibid.*, III, p. 26. Yearning of the wood: Ibn Sa'd, I/1, p. 125, ll. 10 f. She-camel: *ibid.*, I/1, p. 124. *Miskhāt* 1275 f., 1283, 1284 f., 1287 f., 1298.

rupted tradition, we know that they are not true. Further, we do not concede that all those wondrous things come under the heading of miracles. Some of them may come under this heading, but their reporters are few, and no certainty can be derived from their reporting. These things parallel the extraordinary deeds reported of Zoroaster and his ilk, yet all the Muslims maintain that these reports are false.

**Theologians reply.**

We know from practice that a great mass of people cannot possibly ascribe strange and wondrous things to a man to whom nothing of the kind has ever happened. The people who produced those *ḥadīṯ* stories are evidently neither enemies nor friends, but just Muslims, and, therefore, they must know from the religion of Muhammad that lying is prohibited; how, then, will they expose themselves to the great chastisement by fabricating traditions? We do not know how many reporters of Zoroaster and others there were at the beginnings of their faiths, but we know the Muslims were numerous from the beginning of the faith of Islam.

Perhaps these reports were not carried by transmission
92 because the witnesses of each one were few. Although each case may be doubtful, decision depends on the total effect. For assumptions, if continuous, lead to categorical judgments about what they cumulatively confirm. This applies to things empirical.

**I say:**

There is room for speculation in this matter. Namely, many a person will, for worldly goals and motives, do things for which, as he most assuredly knows, the founder of his respective religion has threatened severe punishment in the hereafter. This belief will not prevent a man from perpetrating that forbidden evil. Such is the case of the adulterer, wine-imbiber, and slanderer. In the quest for victory over opponents, human nature will urge the fabrication of reports favoring one's religion. Ignoring the prohibition against lying, a man will sometimes fabricate such a report in the [mistaken] belief that he will merit reward therefor. It may also be fabricated by one who joined a faith opportunistically—without inner conviction but rather in the quest for success, like many who nowadays join the faith of Islam in order to prevail over rivals, although they are not believers by conviction. If your assertion were true, no Muslim would ever have fabricated a false tradition; the contrary, however, is the case.

The report of such extraordinary happenings, assuming its veracity, may still have arisen as a result of subterfuge or collusion among some of Muhammad's companions; similar assertions are sometimes made about the traditions of Zoroaster and others like him.

The assertion "we do not know the number of the carriers of a tradition on behalf of Zoroaster at the beginning of his faith" is invalid, for the time of his rise is known; the Magians were then in a great kingdom and substantially more numerous than the Muslims were at the time of the Prophet.

Only one lacking familiarity with historical and biographical works can doubt this.

It is not necessarily true that a number of assumptions lead to a rational conclusion: they may do so with empirical data, but, on the other hand, may not do so with inductions. When the particulars of judgment are untransmitted, then the sum total of those particulars, that is, the universal judgment, is not always transmitted; it may or may not be. Reason decides what recourse to take in this matter. After hearing the individual accounts of miraculous deeds, the opponent does
not conclude that Muhammad performed any miracles. For 93
the sum total, that is, the performance of miracles is not transmitted in the case of Muhammad. If it were transmitted about Muhammad, the opponent would not be able to deny it, just as he can not deny that Muhammad existed and claimed prophethood. Indeed, there are many passages in the glorious Koran showing that Muhammad performed no miracle.
There is, for example, the verse:

> Nothing has prevented Us sending the signs, but that the people of long ago counted them false;[100]

or the verse:

> Why are not signs from his Lord sent down to him? Say:

100. Koran 17: 61 (59).

> 'signs are with God only and I am only a clear warner, hath it not sufficed them that we have sent down to thee the Book?'[101]

or the verse:

> Those who have disbelieved say: Why has not a sign been sent down to him from his Lord? Thou art only a warner, and for every people there is a guide.[102]

There are also the verses:

> They say "we shall not give thee credence till thou causest for us to bubble up from the earth a spring; or until thou hast a garden of palm and vine, and thou causest in the midst of it rivers to gush forth; or until thou causest the heaven to fall upon us in fragments as thou hast said, or thou producest God and the angels assenting; or until thou hast a house of ornamental work, or thou ascendest into the heaven; nor shall we give credence to thy ascent until thou bringest down to us a writing which we may read." Say: "Glory be to my Lord! am I anything but a human being sent as a messenger?"[103]

In another passage it says:

> they said: "O God, if this be the truth from Thee, rain upon us stones from the heaven, or come to us with a painful punishment; but God was not one to punish them whilst thou wert amongst them."[104]

And there is the verse:

> He is but a crazy poet, or let him bring a miracle as did those of olden time.[105]

It is clear to every sensible person that if Muhammad had brought forward a sign showing he was right he would have said to them:

> Why do you ask me about signs? I have brought them to you;

and he would not have said:

---

101. Koran 29: 49–50.
102. Koran 13: 8(7).
103. Koran 17: 92–95.
104. Koran 8: 32–33.
105. Koran 21: 5.

> Nothing has prevented Us from sending the signs but that the people of long ago counted them false;[106]

nor:

> God was not one to punish them whilst thou wert amongst them.[107]

Several passages in the Koran demonstrate this, but there is no need to examine them here. The imām Fakhr al-Dīn al-Rāzī answered all similar queries with the very same reply he gave to the problems of the annunciation of mysteries.[108]

**Proof Four.** 94

There were annunciations about the advent of Muhammad in the books of the prophets before his time. For Muhammad claimed that he had been mentioned in the Torah and in the Gospel, as witness the verse:

> who follow the messenger, the gentile prophet whom they find mentioned in their Torah and Gospel;[109]

and also as if quoting Christ:

> announcing the good tidings of a messenger who will come after me, bearing the name Aḥmad;[110]

and further:

> O people of the Book, why do ye disbelieve the signs of God though ye are witnesses;[111]

and:

> Those to whom We have given the Book recognize him as they recognize their own sons.[112]

Of course, if all these assertions had been false, it would have been likely to make Jews and Christians extremely averse to

---

106. Cf. n. 100, above.

107. Cf. n. 104, above.

108. Cf. n. 94, above.

109. Koran 7: 156 (157). Cf. Koran 2: 73. Gentile (*ummī*), someone belonging to a community that had no previous scripture.

110. Koran 61: 6. *Aḥmad,* i.e., the praised one (which is also the meaning of *Muhammad*). This is probably based on confusion of (Greek) *parákl̄etos,* comforter (John 14: 16) and *periklutós,* celebrated. The confusion must have its source in some informants of Muhammad's circle.

111. Koran 3: 63 (70).

112. Koran 6: 20.

accepting them. But it would not befit a sensible person to set out on an action that would deter him from his goal and uselessly thwart his aspiration. This is a general consideration.[113]

Concerning particulars, the Torah contains a passage to the effect that the angel announced to Hagar that Ishmael would be a great man, that his hand would be against every man and every man's hand would be against him, and that he would dwell on the borders of the land of all his brethren. The words *against every man* may mean that his hand would rule over all, or that he would mix with all. Now, it is known that Ishmael and his children were not rulers over most nations, nor did they mix with them except in the age of Islam. But the angel of God does not annunciate evil, violence, and falsehood.[114]

The Torah declares, also, that the Lord said to Moses:

> I will raise them a prophet from among their brethren, like unto thee; and I will put My words in his mouth . . . and whosoever will not hearken unto My words which he shall speak in My name, I will require it of him.[115]

If this prophet were to be of the children of Israel, the text would have said "from among themselves," not "from among their brethren." But the Torah [specifies] no prophet like unto Moses will arise from among the children of Israel,[116] and the annunciation, therefore, refers to a prophet from another people, that is, to Muhammad.

The Torah says, further, that God's might

> came from Sinai, rose from Seir unto them, and shined forth from Mount Paran.[117]

It has been discovered by someone that according to the manu-

---

113. Cf. *Arba'īn*, p. 313. I.e. how could Muhammad put forward such claims if he knew they were false and were bound to alienate the Jews and the Christians.

114. Gen. 16: 12.

115. Deut. 18: 18–19. *I will require it of him* is put here as: *I shall revenge myself upon him.*

116. Deut. 34: 10.

117. Deut. 33: 2.

script of Ibn Kūfī's book *Manāzil Makka,* Mount Paran is in Hejaz.[118]

The author of the book *Ifḥām,* a former Jew who turned 95
against the Jews and embraced Islam, argues that God, in the Torah, says to Abraham:

> And as for Ishmael, I have heard thee; behold I have blessed him, and will make him fruitful, and will multiply him exceedingly.[119]

The expression 'exceedingly' is in the original *bi-m*$^{e}$*'od m*$^{e}$*'od,* and the sum total of the numerical value of its letters is equal to that of the letters in the name Muhammad, which is 92. As this word, which indicates excess, occurs in a verse like this, which extols the honour of Ishmael and his children, it is not surprising that it should contain an allusion to the most powerful of them all.

This, then, is the summary of the arguments derived from the Torah.

The arguments from the other prophetic books are:

In the book of the prophet Habakkuk it is stated that the Holy One comes from Mount Paran, followed by wars and conquest upon the earth.[120]

In the book of the prophet Isaiah the blossoming of the land of Kedar and of the wilderness is mentioned, along with its abundance of water for the chosen people to drink.[121]

In the book of the prophet Ezekiel we learn that a plant will be grounded in the wilderness that will destroy the remnant of the power of the Jews.[122]

In the book of the prophet Zephaniah it says that God will renew the chosen tongue.[123]

---

118. Text: *of Kufi.* But this must be a reference to the collector and calligrapher Ibn al-Kūfī. Cf. Fuat Sezgin, *Geschichte des arabischen Schrifttums* (Leiden, 1967), I, pp. 384 f.

119. Gen. 17: 20. From Samau'al, pp. 32 f.

120. Hab. 3: 3 ff.

121. Isa. 42: 11; 35: 1–2, 6 ff.

122. Ezek. 19: 13–14.

123. Zeph. 3: 9.

It says in the Gospel: I shall send unto you the Paraklet.[124]

They conclude: A fair person will recognize from all this that none but the prophet Muhammad and his people are intended.[125]

### Retort

The imām Fakhr al-Dīn al-Rāzī writes about this in his book *al-Muḥaṣṣal:*[126]

> Either you say that the description of Muhammad occurs in these books in detail, i.e., that God explained that in a certain year there would come a man from a certain city of such and such description, and know you that he is My messenger; or else you do not say this but say that God explained this in a general statement without specifying the time, place, and description.
>
> If you claim the former, it is false, because we find the Torah and the Gospel void thereof. It cannot be said that the Jews and the Christians distorted these two books, because we say that these two books were well-known east and west, and in such a case, like in that of the Koran, distortion is precluded.
>
> If, however, you claim the latter, then, even if it be supported, it does not indicate prophethood but only points to the appearance of an excellent, noble man; and if it indicates prophethood, it does not point to the prophethood of Muhammad for it may be that another man was the one announced therein.

96 **I say:**

This is a general objection to the use of particular scriptural passages. It cannot serve as an objection to the general argument. But what can be said about the general argument is rather that the act would be defeating its purpose, if Muhammad, when addressing Jews and Christians on the subject, had stated that he had been mentioned in the Torah and in the Gospel. Possibly no Jews or Christians were present when he

124. Cf. n. 110, above.

125. Cf. chap. 15 in Māwardī's *A'lām al-nubūwa* (Cairo, 1935).

126. *Muḥaṣṣal,* pp. 153 f.

recited these verses to the people, and he thought the word would not spread and reach them; or perhaps he made the statement after he became strong, and disregarded their denial; or it is possible that it was from a favor-currying scriptuary who pretended to embrace Islam and whom Muhammad considered truthful that he had heard that he was mentioned in these two books. This is not unlike the report in history books about a Jew coming to the chieftain of the Zanj,[127] in the time of al-Muhtadi[128] and al-Mu'tamid,[129] prostrating himself and saying: we find thee mentioned in the Torah. Many a Muslim scholar inveighed against tales and reports emanating from such people.[130] It is also possible that after Muhammad's death some of the hypocrites purposely added this to the Koran intending thereby to impair the faith. This, indeed, is believed to be true by those who maintain that the particulars of the Koran verses have not been ascertained by transmission. But it is possible, too, that this statement was made for a different reason—one we cannot ascertain.

In discussing particular passages, we may also say that we do not concede that the biblical verse

> his hand against every man and every man's hand against him[131]

refers to the multitude of nations; it refers, rather, to all of Ishmael's brethren and his clan, and "his dwelling on the borders of the territory of all his brethren" states it clearly.

The expression *your brethren*[132] in addressing the Israelites usually means one from their midst, and the reference to a prophet whom God will raise from amongst the brethren of the Israelites means that he will be from their midst. There are

---

127. Negro slaves imported to Iraq to work saltpeter mines revolted under a pretender in 869–883. The story is found in Ṭabarī's *Annales* III 1760. Cf. Alexandre Popovic, *'Alī b. Muhammad, la révolte des slaves à Basra*, Paris, 1965 (Sorbonne thesis), p. 131.

128. Caliph, 869–870.

129. Caliph, 870–892.

130. I.e., against Israīlīyāt, lore supposedly of Jewish origin.

131. Gen. 16: 12.

132. Deut. 18: 15.

rare exceptions to this usage; for example, the passage

> your brethren the children of Esau.[133]

The passage

> [and] there hath not arisen a prophet since in Israel like unto Moses[134]

means: one in direct communication with God on every subject, with no intermediary.

97 In reference to the verse

> [God] came from . . . Mount Paran[135]

the Torah says that Moses and the Israelites stopped at Paran where God addressed Moses several times. Now, even if we concede Paran to be a place name in Hijaz (though the tradition about that is weak) still a place outside Hijaz had been named that also, and some persons' names indicate provenance from that place. Among them is the author of the book *Dīwān al-Adab*,[136] and he is the best known of those who asserted it was in the Hijaz. Further, he who reads the passages in question in their context realizes that the whole discourse concerns Israelites specifically, not what others may have in common with them. Furthermore, the words *came, rose, shined forth* all relate to a matter of the past, not to something expected in the future. If the passages are interpreted to represent expectation, they are metaphorical, not to be taken literally. Also, it would be improper that the intent of the wording "God's might came from Sinai" be to report about the past, and be followed by the wording *rose, shined forth* as an announcement about what is to come. If the opinion was accurate that the passages "came from Sinai," "rose from Seir," and "shined forth from Mount Paran" alluded to the prophethood of Moses, Jesus, and Muhammad, respectively, then the following passage "and came from the myriads holy" would be an allusion to a fourth religion—a conclusion no Muslim has reached.

---

133. Deut. 2: 4.

134. Deut. 34: 10. Cf. *Guide* Book II ch. 35.

135. Deut. 33: 2.

136. Perhaps Abū Ibrāhīm Isḥāq al-Fārābī (d. 350/961); cf. *GAL*, I, p. 128; Suppl. I, p. 195.

The argument about the numerical value of words put forth by the author of the book *Ifḥām*[137] is too unsound to be discussed seriously. The word whose numerical value is 92, for example, occurs in a number of passages not concerned with Ishmael. If the prophetic books were interpreted by computing the numerical value of their letters, the texts would lose their direct meanings, and he who quotes them would be confronting objections against him rather than gaining points favoring him.

In the matter of adducing passages from the books of the Israelite prophets, the distortion in such passages will be evident to those who will read their books and perceive their contexts, and it will become clear that no argument can emerge from them at all.

The Paraklet mentioned in the Gospel was sent to the apostles after the ascension of Jesus. This is well-known in their traditions, and all the Christians agree thereupon. The Gospel contains the injunction not to be misled by a claimant to prophethood after Christ.[138]

The quotations from the Torah and other scriptures were 98
translated into Arabic inexactly, and were considerably distorted. This is clear to anybody who knows those scriptures.

It is because of these and similar objections that the imām Fakhr al-Dīn al-Rāzī does not rely on arguments which adduce annunciations from the earlier scriptures but relegates such arguments to the category of possible supplements to the argument about the Koran. It was this Koran argument on which he relied exclusively in the book *al-Muḥaṣṣal.*[139]

**Proof Five.**

Defective man is man at his lowest, the vulgar; man as a saint, perfect but unable to perfect others, is the middle stage; and the highest level of man is the prophet, perfect in himself and able to perfect others. Further, this perfection and perfecting are considered to have two aspects—theoretical and

---

137. Samau'al al-Maghribī.

138. Cf. n. 110, above. Matt. 7: 15–20.

139. *Ma'ālim,* pp. 153 f.

practical. The major perfection in the speculative disciplines is considered to be to know God. The major perfection in the practical disciplines is considered to be to obey God. The higher the attainment in perfecting others in these two domains, the higher the stage of prophethood.[140]

At the time of Muhammad's advent the world was full of unbelief. For example, the Jews likened God to his creation, slandered the prophets, and distorted the Torah; the Christians distorted the Gospel and viewed God as one of a Trinity, with Christ as the son of God, and God dwelling in him and uniting with him; the Magians postulated two deities and a struggle between them, and allowed marriage with sisters and daughters; the Arabs worshipped idols and considered pillage, raiding, killing daughters, and so on, lawful; the Indians, Chinese, Turks, Sudanese, and Berbers all practiced equally evident paganism. When God sent Muhammad to call
99 people to the true faith, the world turned from the false to the true, from unbelief to belief, from falsehood to verity, and from darkness to light. These categories of unbelief and paganism became extinct and disappeared in most countries of the central region of the inhabited world. The tongues of men rang out in praise of one God; minds became enlightened by knowing Him, and men turned, to the extent possible, from love for the world to love for the Lord. If prophecy consists in perfecting those defective in speculative power and practical capacity, and if we accept that this result has been achieved more fully and clearly with the advent of Muhammad than it was with the advents of Moses and Jesus, then we must realize that Muhammad is the lord of the prophets and the model of the pure.

We said that this effect was more fully achieved as a result of his rise, because the call of Moses was confined to the Israelites who were but few in number in comparison with the community of Muhammad. As for Jesus, his true call did not survive him at all, and later Christians teach sheer ignorance and outright heresy. It appears, then, that the people of the

140. *Ma'ālim*, pp. 94 ff.

world benefited by Muhammad's call more than the various communities did by the call of all the other prophets. It follows that Muhammad is superior to the rest of the prophets.

This is the method mentioned by the imām Fakhr al-Dīn al-Rāzī in the book *Ma'ālim*,[141] and he gave it preference over other methods of argumentation.

**I say**

that Rāzī's division of mankind into the vulgar, the saints, and the prophets is not comprehensive because it omits the learned. Also there is room for speculation about each division in his interpretation.

It is not the prophet who is the perfect man, able to perfect others by addressing them on behalf of God; it is, rather, the learned, the investigator who can rightly be believed to be perfect and able to perfect others although he is not a prophet in the sense that we have sought to establish. If [Rāzī] meant all the [prophetic] qualities of perfection, or most of them, we preclude the achievement thereof by any human being. But apart from that, we will not concede that [Muhammad] added to the knowledge of God and to obedience to Him anything more than was found in the earlier religions.

The assertion that the Jews liken God to His creations is inadmissible; on the contrary, their religion and creed are the denial of anthropomorphism. Any of them who deviates and is at variance with this is of no consequence.

The claim that statements expressive of anthropomorphism occur in their Torah and in the books and lives of their prophets can be countered by stating that the Muslims' books, 100
especially those of tradition, such as the *Ṣaḥīḥs*[142] and others, contain expressions of anthropomorphism in greater number and more definitely than those of the Jews.

If one says that the Muslims interpreted such texts in a way which eliminates literal meaning, we say: the Jews too interpreted their own texts in a more plausible manner and one that is superior to that of the Muslims. Indeed, the Mus-

---

141. *Ibid.*, p. 110.

142. Cf. n. 34, above.

lims maintain, on the authority of their tradition-transmitters, authentic stories of anthropomorphism and corporeality that the sound mind will not accept, and that cannot be interpreted —except, perhaps, arbitrarily. But not all the Muslims, especially the early authorities on tradition, seem to accept the fact that there are difficulties raised by such stories. Many of them have declared that their deity is a shape with limbs and parts that can move, go up and down, rest, stay, and touch; that the righteous will embrace him in this world and in the hereafter; and that they will visit Him and He will visit them.

One of them said: Excuse me from talking of pudenda and the beard and ask me about what is beyond that. They said: He is a body, not like the bodies, flesh unlike flesh, blood that is not like blood. One of them says that God is hollow from the top to His chest, the rest is compact, and that He has thick black hair that is short and curly, hand and foot, head, tongue, eyes, ears, and other limbs. Their discussion on the subject is extensive. Were it not for the beneficial impact that the works of the philosophers have upon some of them, their [religious] texts would not preclude the belief that God is a body, though, as asserted by the verse *There is nothing anything like Him,*[143] a body unlike other bodies. Whoever wants to learn the anthropomorphic traditions may turn to the special books on the subject and find awesome things. These traditions are so numerous, that although each story is reported on a single authority, the sum total would amount to the tenet of anthropomorphism as a continuously transmitted tradition, and not a mere series of individual reports. Some interpreters said that heretics feigning belief in Islam reported these stories as a means to impugn the faith. This is possible in some cases but is unfair in most, because their reporters, whose sound creed is not doubted, are widely known for their piety and probity, and the Muslims rely on their reports and the reports of others like them in most of their jurisprudence.[144]

---

143. Koran 42: 9 (11).
144. Cf. I. Goldziher, *Vorlesungen über den Islam* (Heidelberg, 1910),

It is, also, inadmissible to charge the Jews with slandering the prophets and distorting the Torah; this has been discussed previously. 101

The Christian tenet and discussion of God as a Trinity is well-known, and though this is a current expression among the Christians they are, nevertheless, monotheists, maintaining that God has no partners. Their tenet of trinity with unity of substance is like the tenet of those Muslims who postulate eternal additional attributes contained in one divine substance.

The Christian tenet of incarnation and union may be interpreted in a way that precludes a belief of error and ignorance, just as Islamic anthropomorphic allusions are interpreted away by Muslims—who can claim no superiority over the Christians in this respect.

The charge that the Christians distorted the Gospel is without proof and is not conceded by them.

The Zoroastrians do not postulate that there are two deities struggling for supremacy. They teach, rather, that God is one, and that there is a good force, Yazdan, and an evil force, Ahriman. Among the Zoroastrians, the Manichaeans and Daisanites[145] teach that those forces are light and darkness. Their permissiveness about marriage with sisters and daughters is not a rationally inadmissible practice; the prohibition of such marriages is one point of the revealed precepts, and this kind of marriage has become disreputable among us because most religions known to us forbid it.

The worship of idols is in existence to this day among the

---

chap. 3; A. S. Tritton, *Muslim Theology* (London, 1947), p. 48; al-Ash'arī, *Maqālāt al-Islāmīyīn*, ed. H. Ritter (2d ed.; Wiesbaden, 1963), pp. 34, 207, 209; Shahrastānī, *Milal*, ed. W. Cureton (London, 1846), pp. 75–79, section on the *Mushabbiha*.

145. Medieval Islamic books on religions and heresies list this group which no longer existed by the time of Ibn Kammūna. It had been a syncretistic group combining Christian and dualistic notions, insisted on scholarship and scientific pursuits. The founder, Bardaiṣan, lived in Syria in 154–222 (?), wrote Christian poems in Syriac, but was excommunicated for his unorthodox tenets. Chrysippus (f. p. 35, n. 25) had held (Plutarch, *De Stoic.* ch. 22) similar views. Cf. p. 53, n. 19.

Chinese, Turks, Indians, and others. True, it ceased among the Arabs with the coming of Muhammad. It has been said, however, that the Black Stone was one of the idols that was in the Ka'ba, but that, unlike the other idols, it was not removed. Muslims to this day seek closeness to God through kissing and touching the Black Stone, which is a kind of worship. The idolators do not believe idols create heaven and earth; no sensible person does. But they do feel that idol worship brings one closer to God. We are informed by the Koran that they said: this is our way to bring us near to God in intimacy.[146]

102 Submission to God is enjoined upon man in the other faiths, also. *If* it is said that what non-Muslims do in their prayer, fasting, and other specific rites is *no* worship, for worship is that which is done in accordance with God's commands and is not abrogated by another religion, and that which the non-Muslims do does not come under this category, then we say that you cannot prove that it does not come under this category unless the prophethood of Muhammad is established first. But if you establish it in this fashion, you are in the throes of circular reasoning, which is absurd.

Further, how can Muhammad be called the most perfect man in practical wisdom when Muslim kings, in carrying out government and maintaining law and order in the polity, are compelled to violate the religious law in stipulations on punishment and retaliation, and so on? If the law of Islam were acted upon without any alteration, the regime would be upset, and people's blood and wealth would be forfeited unjustly. This is no secret to anyone acquainted with Muslim jurisprudence and with the evil and corruption the people sink into.

---

146. Koran 39: 4. Two MSS continue: "It is reported that a Qarmaṭian said as he was crushing the Black Stone with his mace and some fragments were coming off it: How long shall we worship this? The Muslims later took the chipped-off fragments, baked them in musk, and restored them to their previous position. This is mentioned by the historians. They assert that the idolators do not believe, etc."

This refers to the seizure of Mecca by the Qarmaṭi sectarians in 317/929 and the return of the Black Stone twenty years later. Cf. *SEI*, s.v. Ka'ba, sec. iii, and s.v. Qarmaṭ; M. J. De Goeje, *Mémoires d'histoire et de géographie orientales*, no. 1 (Leiden, 1886), pp. 100–111.

Thus it becomes clear that there is no proof that Muhammad attained perfection and the ability to perfect others as claimed, nor that anything mentioned on this point has been proved at all—for example, the allegation that the world turned from falsehood to truth, from lie to veracity, from darkness to light, and so on. Yet precisely this has been the subject of dispute.[147]

That is why, to this day we never see anyone converting to Islam unless in terror, or in quest of power, or to avoid heavy taxation, or to escape humiliation, or if taken prisoner, or because of infatuation with a Muslim woman, or for some similar reason. Nor do we see a respected, wealthy, and pious non-Muslim well versed in both his faith and that of Islam, going over to the Islamic faith without some of the aforementioned or similar motives.

A multitude of followers and the diffusion of a cause in many lands do not prove a claim. A student of history will observe many cases wherein an individual, even a slave, revolting single-handedly, will enjoy success, and attract many thousands of followers.

When Musaylima, Aswad al-'Absī, Ṭulayḥa, and Sajāḥ 103
claimed prophethood, each was followed by a multitude of Arabs who believed in him or her.[148] Were it not for Abū Bakr's perseverance in fighting the "secessionists" they might have succeeded. In the time of the prophet a great mass of people were hypocrites and many became apostates; among them were 'Abdallah b. Sa'd, the prophet's secretary, and

147. Directed against the Fifth proof as formulated by Rāzī in *Ma'ālim*, pp. 94, 110.

148. Musaylima, contemporary of Muhammad, who claimed prophethood and was defeated after Muhammad's death (cf. n. 34, above). Aswad al-'Absī, a Yamani chieftain led a revolt in the Prophet's last year. He claimed to be a soothsayer on behalf of God. He was slain before the Prophet's death. Ṭulayḥa, a tribal leader, fought the Prophet, then converted to Islam but joined the revolt in Central Arabia and declared himself prophet. Defeated, he reverted to Islam and later took part in the conquest of Persia. Sajāḥ, originally a Christian woman, led a revolt against Islam and its Medina center, united with Musaylima whom she married. It seems that she survived defeat and ended her days in peace.

'Ubaydallah b. Jaḥsh, who, after migrating to Ethiopia, embraced Christianity and died a Christian.[149]

How, since the dominion of idol-worshippers and fire-worshippers continued for thousands of years in numberless countries throughout the world, can a multitude of followers be proof of a claim?

I found they had no rebuttal to these arguments beyond the claim that the Islamic faith obviously excels over other faiths, and that it combines a maximum quantity and quality of perfection not attained by any other known faith. But he who, in rancour, makes this claim will never be able to present proof of it.[150]

**Proof Six.**

A number of points that can only combine in a prophet did so in Muhammad. These consist of two categories: one pertaining to the senses and the other pertaining to the intellect.

---

149. His widow was returned from Ethiopia to become the Prophet's wife. She was the daughter of Abū Sufyān, the Meccan leader.

150. A suggested Muslim defense appears in two MSS: "Kissing the black stone is not worship. For by worship of a thing one understands [there to be] the belief that that thing may be helpful or harmful. Other conditions are attached to the belief which also are not fulfilled by mere kissing with the view to approach God. That is why it is reported that 'Umar said: I kiss thee but know thou art neither helpful nor harmful.

"As to the matter of political organization without Islamic law, considering the law of Islam as just does not mean insistence upon punishing someone who may be innocent or punishment in a doubtful case, as usually practiced by the rulers.

"As to Islam being embraced by some for worldly considerations, it does not contradict the fact that others believe in Islam without these considerations, such as those early believers who were drawn by hearing the Koran and by other admonitions.

"We find close to our time that a person embraced Islam and began to violate the stipulations of his former faith.

"The multitude of followers and the spread of a cause do become an argument when they coincide with miracles.

"I have dwelt so extensively on the doubts of the opponents in this matter and on other points lest I should fail to comply with what I laid down as a condition at the beginning of the book: to reach thoroughness by giving the argument of both sides."

The former, the sensible, is divided into three parts: matters external to himself; matters within himself; matters concerning his character traits.[151]

Matters external to himself pertain to the miracles appearing through him.

Matters within himself include the light that was passed from generation to generation until it came forth into the world, the seal between his shoulders, and his known build and shape, indicative, by virtue of physiognomy, of his prophethood.[152]

The points concerning his character traits refer to the facts that: no falsehood and no meanness could be committed against him; no terror could force him to run from his enemies; he was affectionate, compassionate, and generous toward his community; the world had no attraction for him; he was eloquent and remained gracious to the end of his life; he was very 104
disdainful with worldly and wealthy people, and very humble with the poor, unfortunate, and pious. He combined all of these qualities and attained the acme in each. This has not happened to any other human being.

The second category, that is, matters pertaining to the intellect, consists of six groups:

Group 1.

Muhammad appeared in a tribe made up of unlearned men, travelled from his land to Syria only twice, briefly, and is not known to have studied under any master. Yet his vast knowledge of God, His attributes, works, names, and rulings, and his awareness of some of the ancient narratives and histories of earlier generations, were all unattainable except with divine guidance.

Group 2.

Some forty years of his life must have passed without his delving into any of these scholarly subjects, or his enemies would surely have mentioned it. He then pursued all of them

---

151. *Arbaʿīn*, pp. 309 ff.

152. Light: cf. Andrae, *Die Person Muhammeds*, pp. 319 ff. Seal: cf. Bukhārī I p. 61, n. 40, end; *Miskhāt* 1240, 1242 f.

at once in an idiom uncontested by both the ancients and the moderns, and *that* was possible only through inspiration and revelation.

Group 3.

He endured various hardships and troubles in discharging his apostolate, but showed neither flagging nor slackening in the pursuit of his goal and in his perseverance. Nor, when he was victorious over his enemies and came into power, did he change his pattern of asceticism in this life, and his preoccupation with the life to come. An impostor, on the other hand, strives only for worldly success. If he achieves it but does not enjoy it, he seems bent on losing both his life and the life to come, which a sensible person would not do.

Group 4.

His requests were divinely granted. For he said: "O God, treat Muḍar harshly, let them have years like those of Joseph." God then denied rain to them, and when they asked him to intercede for them, he asked for rain to be sent down to them, and it came until they feared drowning in it. They turned to him again, asking him to pray that it should rain only to the extent necessary. He then said: "O God, around us, not upon us, O God, upon the mountains and deep valleys." And that tribulation, consequently, was repealed.[153]

When he wrote an epistle to the Persian king, the latter tore it up, and sent the prophet a handful of dust. The prophet then said: "O God, tear up his kingdom." And he said to his companions: "He sent to us the dust of his land, and this indi-
105 cates mastery over his land." And it was as he said.[154]

Referring to 'Utba b. Abī Lahab he said: "O God, make one of thy dogs master over him." A lion later tore 'Utba to pieces.[155]

About 'Abdallāh b. 'Abbās he said: "O God, make him

---

153. Bukhārī, II, p. 231. A prototype of the story is the account of Ḥoni Hamme'aggel (first century B.C.) in the talmudic treatise Ta'aniṯ, p. 23*a*. Muḍar: northern Arabs. Cf. Bukhārī I p. 257 f; Miskhāt 1282 f.

154. Ibn Ḥanbal, III, p. 447.

155. Abū Lahab, half-brother of Muhammad's father; foe of the Prophet; mentioned in the Koran (111: 1) in an imprecation.

wise in the faith, and teach him the interpretation." 'Abdallāh then became the chief of exegetes.[156]

When the unbelievers reached the cave the Prophet recited over them, while they were looking at the cave and did not see him, the verse:

> We have set before them a barrier, and behind them a barrier, and We have thrown a cover over them, so they do not clearly see.[157]

As the Prophet emerged from the cave, one of the unbelievers came close to him and the Prophet said: "O earth, take him." Thereupon the legs of that unbeliever's horse became submerged in the soil.

Group 5.

The annunciation of the prophet's advent is contained in the Torah and the Gospel, which has been discussed above.

Group 6.

He announced mysteries; also discussed above.

**The Retort**

to this argumentation is that most of it is based on individual reporting, and is not conducive to certitude. The admirable aspects of the prophet that it mentions, were we to concede the truth of the reports about them, present a weak argument for prophethood. At the most, they may indicate that greater virtue distinguished the man from other people.[158] But how does this indicate prophethood? Consider the impressive stories attesting to the characters of great sages whom men have set as examples for themselves in this world and in the hereafter. These sages, moreover, are reported to have possessed knowledge of exact sciences whereas no such report about Muhammad exists.

The duration of his trip to Syria was not too brief for him to learn the modicum of narratives, and so on, adduced in the Koran; indeed, it was more time than he needed. Nor is it certain that he was not a disciple of some master.

156. Ibn Sa'd, I:2, p. 120. 'Abdallāh (619–687) became a famous authority on and transmitter of numerous traditions.

157. Koran 36: 8 (9). Cf. 9: 40.

158. Cf. *Muḥaṣṣal*, p. 154 l. 4.

His knowledge of the essence and the attributes of the Creator was not something unknown before his mission; the pagan Arabs knew this, as their poetry and stories attest.

That he plunged into these subjects all at once is not likely; but perhaps he was delving secretly. Originally he urged the religion of Abraham upon the Arabs, and then he pro-
106 ceeded gradually to urge upon them a faith of his own, altering it constantly in accordance with changing situations. How, then can it be said that his preaching emerged suddenly, without gradation?

The failure to contest the Koran has been discussed earlier.

The statement that he did not change his ascetic pattern after he became powerful is supercilious. For example, after he came into power he allowed himself to marry an unlimited number of women but did not permit the other men of his community to marry more than four women. He married by formula of gift, without dower, guardian, or witnesses. If he desired to wed a married woman, her husband was forced to divorce her, in the same manner that, for example, Zayd divorced Zaynab because the messenger of God desired and then married her. He had the right to marry a woman before the completion of the stipulated waiting period, and he did not consider himself obligated to observe equity, as defined by the best legists, among his wives. He ruled that he was more entitled to a share of the booty than the believers, and set aside Ṣafīya for himself; and he ruled, further, that he had exclusive right to a fifth of the booty.[159]

He would send out his raiding parties merely to pillage the wealth and goods of the infidels.

He accumulated nine wives and many concubines, and one of the latter bore him a child. He loved perfume, and used much of it. He did not neglect partaking of foods he liked. It is reported that he would say: if you cook in a pot, put into it much gherkin. He would eat cucumber with fresh dates and

159. Koran 33: 49–52. Zaynab: *ibid.*, verse 37. Ṣafīya, the Prophet's wife, was a Jewish prisoner who received freedom as her dowry. She lived for some thirty years after the Prophet's death.

salt, and enjoyed melon and grapes. Often he would eat so many grapes that his spittle got into his beard. His favourite food was meat: meat of game—bird, for example—and he would eat broth with meat and pumpkin, along with bread, butter, and water; and he would sip milk with dates. He liked the leg and shoulder of mutton, gurkin in the pot, the gourd, date vinegar condiment, and pressed vegetables like endive, citronelle, and the garden parsley.[160]

How can such a man be called ascetic? Moreover, seizure of power and autocracy are the world's greatest pleasures, and it is not surprising that he gave up other pleasures but retained these.

That his requests were granted by heaven emanates from individual reporting.

The annunciation of his advent and his disclosure of mysteries have been discussed before.

### The Muslims Could Say

we have mentioned these points for their cumulative 107
effect, not for the sake of each argument.[161] If you deny the

---

160. Cf. Bukhārī, III, pp. 493 ff. (section Aṭ'ima, on foods); and L. Zolondek's *Book XX of al-Ghazālī's Ihyā 'Ulūm al-Dīn* (Leiden, 1963), esp. pp. 30 ff.

161. MS Tehran adds: "Even if the report of each separate tradition emanates from only one individual, it still may be valid.

"If the Prophet had studied in Syria or had been the disciple of some master, this would have been mentioned by his enemies in his own time.

"The ignorance of the pagan Arabs, except a few of them, is well known.

"Muhammad plunged suddenly into the *principles* of the faith, not its ramifications.

"His asceticism means that in his heart he abandoned the love of the world; the specifics on forbidden marriages and so on do not impugn him, especially as he was able to combine the two aspects [asceticism and marriage].

"Taking the infidels' wealth, in the repugnant manner described, was a kind of obligatory holy war, conducted not for acquisition of wealth, but to strengthen the faith and break the power of the infidels.

"What was said about food was meant to show the lack of pomposity and the simplicity of the prophet, not his gluttony.

cogency of the sum total of our characterization of Muhammad as an entity, we, unworried by your denial, shall claim that it is self-evident.

Anyone[162] who makes a point of reading the Koran and the traditions, and strengthens this by practicing the Prophet's directives about acts of worship which have a purifying effect upon hearts;

who sees how right the Prophet was in saying "He who acts upon his knowledge will be granted by God the legacy of knowing what he knew not"; in saying "help a tyrant, and you make him your master"; in saying "if a man and his worries become one worry, God spares him the worries of this world and the next";[163] and in other utterances of wisdom and morality;

that person who considers the divine support granted to the prophet, and how the uncouth Arab looking upon his noble face, could say "by God, this is not the face of a liar,"[164] while another man trusted the prophet's oath when the latter said, "Yes, by God, God sent me as prophet" in answer to his, "I adjure thee by God, is it God that sent you as prophet?";[165]

and he who considers how many nations followed Muhammad, how his cause spread, how divine mercy embraced men upon his advent, and the justice of His law,

he would see therein sufficient evidence of Muhammad's veracity and prophethood.

**But**

this is an intuitive approach that may not be open to

---

"Still, in employing this method, it was not intended to point to each of these matters separately but to their cumulative impact."

162. For the following passage, cf, *Munqiḏ*, p. 43 bottom.

163. Ibn Māja, *Sunan,* sec. "al-Intifā' bi-l-'ilm." Muh. b. Abdallāh al-Khaṭīb al-Tibrizī, *Mishkāt,* trans. James Robson (Lahore, 1963), i, pp. 60 f: If anyone makes the care of his eternal welfare the sum total of his cares, God will protect him from worldly cares; but if he has a variety of cares consisting of matters related to this world, God will not be concerned in which of its *wādī*'s he perishes.

164. Dārimī, *Sunan,* sec. "Istīḏān 4.

165. Bukhārī, I, pp. 26 f.

verification by those who reject it because they themselves do not feel that kind of intuition.

One might say:

How can Muhammad's religion be true, despite the extensive continuous tradition of the two communities, Jews and Christians, each claiming that its religion will last to the day of resurrection? Had Moses or Jesus announced that his religion was discontinuous, this would have been transmitted along with the fundamentals of his religion, and Jews and Christians would be unable to deny it. Had either commanded his believers to observe his religion absolutely, without any reference to temporariness or eternity, no prescribed act in accordance with his religion would be incumbent more than once, for such an absolute command does not provide for more than that. Of course, that is not the case in the faiths of Moses and Jesus. If either had announced that his religion was permanent, and it had proved to be untrue, one might conclude 108
that Muhammad's religion might not last forever despite his statement that it would. Yet no Muslim will affirm this.

We should say: there is no choice except to deny the veracity of the transmission of the Jews and the Christians. But you are acquainted with the discussion on this subject.

Many arguments were raised, and replies given. This subject bears further investigation, but I do not propose adding to what I have mentioned.

I ask God for guidance, protection, good conclusion, mercy, and that I may be placed by Him with those gaining eternal happiness and safety from His punishment. Praise be to God, the Lord of the worlds, and His blessing over His chosen ones and the prophets He favored.

# *Index*